What are we thinking?

WHAT ARE WE THINKING?

REFLECTIONS ON CHURCH AND
SOCIETY FROM SOUTHERN AFRICAN
METHODISTS

Editors: Dion Forster and Wessel Bentley

What are we Thinking? Reflections on Church and Society from Southern African Methodists

ISBN: 978 1 919883 52 6

Published by The Methodist Publishing House
4 Shannon Street, Salt River 7925, Cape Town, South Africa

First published December 2008
Designed by Electric Book Works (www.electricbookworks.com)
Set in Garamond Premier Pro and Fontin Sans

CONTENTS

EDITOR'S INTRODUCTION

The idea for this book grew out of a conversation with Bishop Ivan Abrahams, the Presiding Bishop of the Methodist Church of Southern Africa. One afternoon he and I sat in Christ Church College, Oxford, speaking about the richness of our Southern African Methodist heritage. As we talked we celebrated the blessing and diversity of our Methodist Connexion. The Methodist Church of Southern Africa covers a geographical area that spans 6 nations (Botswana, Mozambique, Swaziland, Lesotho, Namibia, and South Africa). Within the denomination there is a veritable rainbow of cultures and age groups – not to mention the divergent theological perspectives and styles of worship. When you mix the Wesleyan passion for Christian perfection with such diversity and a rich social history, the outcome is quite remarkable to say the least!

In the weeks following that conversation I thought how sad it was that we did not have a resource such as a book or a journal that could capture and reflect the blessing of our theological diversity. So, early one morning, I emailed a number of 'emerging' scholars with the following idea: each one was to write a chapter for a book. The only requirement was that their chapter should reflect a clear position on some theological or social issue about which they felt passionate. Many responded enthusiastically to the challenge and so this book began to take shape.

In the pages of this book a variety of topics has been considered. Some chapters deal with theological issues (such as the notion of theological truth, approaches to theology, and the use of metaphor in theology and scripture); others consider more practical matters (such as economics and the Christian faith, youth development, and crafting an authentically

African liturgical tradition); while still others consider some of the topical issues of our time and context (such as the Church and persons of a same-sex orientation, gender issues, and issues of the environment).

This book has two simple aims:

1. To present a compilation of 'position papers' by Methodist scholars that reflect some of the issues that Southern African Methodists are praying about, talking about, and thinking about. In this sense the book aims to be a *'zeitgeist'* (a 'spirit of the times') reflecting some of our current theological thinking on contemporary issues. You may not necessarily agree with all of the points made here. However, you are encouraged to consider the points that the author makes, to understand why he or she holds the position that is presented, and then go on to form your own opinions and understanding of what you believe in relation to the issue at hand.

2. This leads to the second aim, namely to open the way for our church members to begin to think critically about some contemporary challenges and opportunities that Southern Africa, and the Church in Southern Africa, faces. In this regard the book aims to stimulate prayer, thought, further conversation and ultimately courageous action.

I pray that you will be challenged to grow in your own faith as you read the chapters of this book. Ultimately our common aim is to find the most effective, Christ-like, God-honouring ways of establishing God's Kingdom here on earth.

Dion Forster

CONTRIBUTORS

REV DR WESSEL BENTLEY is a minister at the Glen Methodist Church in Pretoria. He holds a doctorate in Theology, teaches Systematic Theology at John Wesley College and is a part time lecturer in Theological Ethics at the University of South Africa.

REV DR DION FORSTER is a consultant and corporate chaplain in Cape Town. He holds a doctorate in Theology and Science. He was the dean of John Wesley College and has taught New Testament, Greek and Systematic Theology. He is a research associate in the department of New Testament at the University of Pretoria.

REV VUSI VILIKATI is the minister at the Lombardy East Methodist Church in Johannesburg. He holds a Masters degree in Theology and teaches Systematic Theology at John Wesley College.

REV DEBBIE VAN DE LAAR is the minister of the Knysna Methodist Church. She holds a Masters degree in Theology. Her research specialises in helping churches and individual Christians to consider truly Christ-like responses to persons with a same-sex orientation.

REV MANTSO MATSEPE is the minister of one of the MCSA's fastest growing Churches in KwaThema. He is a specialist in liberation and black theologies. He holds a Masters degree in Old Testament.

REV KEVIN LIGHT is a minister 'in exile' from the Methodist Church. He resigned from the MCSA in protest at the Church's unwillingness to allow ministers to conduct the weddings of same-sex couples. Kevin holds an

Honours degree in Pastoral Theology. He is widely regarded as a specialist in postmodernist approaches to mission.

REV ALAN STOREY has been the minister of the Calvary Methodist Church near Johannesburg. From 2009 he will serve the Central Methodist Mission in Cape Town. He holds a Masters degree in Theology and is widely regarded as an expert in issues of social justice.

REV MADIKA SIBEKO was the co-ordinator of training for ordained ministries in the Education for Ministry and Mission Unit of the MCSA. She holds a Masters degree in Theology and is currently pursuing her studies at Cambridge in the UK.

REV JOHN VAN DE LAAR is a consultant and the owner of Sacredise. He holds a Masters degree in Theology and is widely regarded as an expert in worship and liturgy.

REV MOGOMOTSI DIUTLWILENG is the owner and director of Reutlwile, a consulting firm in Human Capital Development with a special focus on Youth Development. He holds an Honours degree in Theology.

FOREWORD

....

Rev Dr Neville Richardson

The contributors to this book are all from a generation much younger than mine, but I am honoured to be associated with them. I am absolutely delighted that this book has been published. In itself it is a visible expression of the 'head, heart and hands' approach of which Dion Forster speaks at the end of his editor's conclusion. Each separate chapter and the book as a whole demonstrate vigorous intellectual energy, passionate Christian commitment, and an invitation to dynamic Christ-inspired activity in various spheres of life.

My enthusiasm for the book is fired by a number of factors. First, there is the variety of authors and topics. While the authors are all connected by virtue of being Methodist ministers, at a vital point in their development – that exciting stage at which they begin to make their mark – they represent many different constituencies. There is a marvellous mix of both race and gender. This mix is witness to the ongoing struggle of the Methodist Church of Southern Africa to 'remain one and undivided' amidst all the forces that have threatened to divide it – and continue to do so.

Second, the variety of topics reflects key points in our social, cultural, economic and political context. I would be very surprised if most of those who pick this book up and scan its contents are not lured into reading one or more of its chapters. I hope that one thing will then lead to another and they will read the whole book.

Third, there is a crying need for up-to-date books that relate the whole gospel to the whole world. The Gospel of John ends by imagining the whole world filled with books about Jesus. Certainly there is a vast publishing industry today, very well marketed, that goes under the name of 'Christian', but which tends to fall within a very narrow theological range, and surely does little to broaden narrow minds! I shudder at how the volume of such material impacts on the forests of the world that are sacrificed for paper. This concern falls directly under the spotlight of the 'green' chapter of this book! As I point this critical finger, however, I am keenly aware of three fingers pointing back at me and those like me who are critical of the huge market in 'narrow theology', but who do little to produce theology that is more contextual and engaged. Therefore, praise God for this book that flies the flag for theology of a wholesome, healthy and helpful kind.

Fourth, the book does not set out to promote one line of thought. It does not aim to indoctrinate us, but rather to challenge us to become thinking Christians in our own contexts. Furthermore, it does not stop with thinking alone – Kevin Light, as his chapter emphasises, would be extremely disappointed if that were the outcome! It explicitly urges us to move beyond thought and debate and to become Christian activists.

While Christian readers of all denominations will be challenged and enriched by this book, the fifth reason for my enthusiasm is that it gives contemporary expression to the spirit of John Wesley. Not only were his interests wide ranging, as are the topics in this book, but he managed to develop that rare and precious mix of a theology that is simultaneously passionate *and* reasonable, both deeply spiritual *and* socially engaged. That is the excellent mix that this book also offers.

I therefore thank Dion Forster and Wessel Bentley most sincerely for the inspiration that brought this book into being and I thank all ten authors for their contributions. Their hard work will surely enrich us all. May this book prove to be a great blessing to many, and may other similar works follow in its wake.

WHOSE TRUTH WILL SET US FREE?

....

Wessel Bentley

I recall seeing a photograph in a newspaper a few years ago depicting a public protest. The protest centred on same-sex relationships. The crowd consisted of a good mix of those opposed to same-sex relationships and those who were campaigning for them. In the middle of the crowd stood a person holding a protest banner that read '*The truth shall set you free! John 8: 32*'. I couldn't quite decide which side of the argument this person represented. The person was not in the middle of either bunch, but stood in a place where it was difficult for someone to classify him as belonging to either perspective. I had to ask myself the question whether this person was campaigning from a Christian background which opposed same-sex relationships based on the numerous Biblical passages that endorse this position. Alternatively, was he advocating an understanding that there is a truth which gives dignity and equality to those who belong to same-sex relationships when they disclose their sexual orientation? We may speculate, but this instance is only one example of the tension in the modern world between perspectives that wish to claim that their position consists of truth – the only truth. We can select almost any ethical, moral or hermeneutical debate and see that there will always be views that are clearly opposed to one another, yet which claim to be the custodians of truth. Religion is no different, not even the Christian faith.

The Christian faith is marred by examples of the rise of factions and doctrinal differences which throughout history have claimed for themselves the status of 'custodians of truth' – even if it has meant that this truth has come at the expense of continued relationship and fellowship with other Christians. The example of the person in the protest group leads us to ask some critical questions about our perception of truth as well as of freedom. What is truth? Which truth is the real truth? Is there such a thing as the real truth? Can truth belong to anyone? If truth leads to freedom, then what does this freedom look like? To use a text such as John 8: 32 in the context of protest suggests that this particular truth is not only an aspect of our faith that should be taken seriously, but that this truth has soteriological implications. If truth leads to freedom, then it must mean that truth is an agent of salvation. Before we speak too loosely about truth, let us consider some aspects of truth that we often take for granted.

THE COMPLEXITY OF THE TERM 'TRUTH'

In order to define truth, we have to note that we are applying an assumed construct to our investigation. In discussing the notion of truth, we are compelled to turn it into the subject of our thinking, therefore transforming it into an observable entity, something that is manageable, or put differently, a notion that can be understood within the context of human consciousness, space and time. The way in which the protester used the concept of truth illustrates how truth exists as a subjective reality which can be shaped by many factors such as context, culture, experience and the like. However, the exercise of defining, analysing or even thinking about truth removes it from its being a purely subjective matter and presents it to the observer as a constant, unchangeable entity – something we assume we can define and describe. The interpretation of this observable truth may still be subject to external influences, but it would be generally assumed that truth becomes an object that can be defined. Even this action negotiates truth's state of truthfulness.

Treating truth as a subject of discussion assumes the existence of another truth, the truth of our observation and interpretation, believing that whatever we may say about truth, *is* the truth, and perhaps even a more realistic version of the truth than the subject of our analysis. This premise serves as an acknowledgment of the flawed nature of our observation and that the conclusions we come to regarding that which we consider to be the truth will never be able to replace truth in its entirety. Truth on the observation table is assumed to be static and unmoved by the dimensions of consciousness, time or space. The best the observer can do is to speak about truth *sub specie temporis*[1], with the understanding that he or she will not be able to harness the full extent of truth.

But even so, speaking about the truth *sub specie temporis* assumes the existence of a singular eternal truth that overshadows, or negates, all other truths. In the realm of religion, especially Christianity, this truth is generally ascribed to God's perspective. And so, as with the protester, righteousness is perceived to be the manifestation of God's truth in the person's life, which is a truth different from that which is accepted by the world. From this perspective, the person who adheres to truth needs to take one of two positions.

God's truth as ultimate truth, fully imparted

The first way is to recognise God's truth as the *only* truth which is fully imparted. Anything else claiming to be the truth is seen to be deceit or a lie that becomes the basis of sin. This notion is not foreign to the Christian tradition. In fact, Biblical tradition reflects many examples of how this understanding of truth is manifested in Judaic and Christian faith.

In the Old Testament this idea is presented in the understanding of retribution. This doctrine finds favour with especially Zion theology, but did not escape the judicial system of Mosaic theology. It argues as follows: 'If God's order is preserved with wisdom, man [sic] is rewarded, but anyone who disturbs the order by his foolishness is punished' (Burden and Prinsloo 1987: 5). God's truth is presented as the only truth that can ensure order within the created realm. In Mosaic theology the emphasis on the covenant between God and Israel suggests that Israel is compelled to ad-

---

1   From the perspective of temporality (not the temporal).

here to God's law in order to be God's people and so become the chosen nation which will reveal God's truth to all nations. A further development in this line of thought suggests that those who adhere to God's will (God's truth), are considered to be filled with God's wisdom and will reap the benefits of God's favour by being blessed with health, wealth and all things good. Poverty and ill health are interpreted as the result of human disobedience and God's dissatisfaction with people's foolishness. This is the theology which is debated in the book of Job where this question forms the crux of the literature: Why do so many righteous people suffer while evil often prospers?

Even Jesus' disciples held this view. Their question to Jesus in John 9: 2, asking who was to blame for the blind man's condition, assumes that God was offended by either this man or his parents. The result was the man's blindness. The disciples' denial of God's truth disturbed the order and therefore God had to act to display God's dissatisfaction. This is not the only example in John's Gospel. Dualism in Johannine literature, illustrated in the use of paradoxical concepts such as 'light and darkness, falsehood and truth, above and below' (Kümmel 1970: 155), conveys the idea that God's perspective presents the only form of living which has true meaning and lasting value. Neo-Platonic influences in Pauline theology, like that described in the tension between *flesh* and *spirit,* suggest that this world and all that it holds cannot present any form of eternal truth, for it is the dwelling place of evil and the embodiment of temporality. Truth belongs to the realm of the eternal. The ability of the individual or community to deny the material and embrace the spiritual serves as a measure for righteousness.

The person or people who are considered to be righteous have reason to claim the moral high ground over others who do not subscribe to their positions. The righteous are considered to be wise for they adhere to the truth which belongs to God and do not have to engage in apologetics. Their truth is nevertheless *the* truth. But there are some questions that need to be asked of this perspective.

Our truth is still subjective, even when truth is divine truth and revealed by God-self. It must be so, for this 'revealed truth' still needs to be interpreted. Even if someone receives the truth in its pristine state, their interpretation of the truth is shaped by their context, experience, world view and beliefs (among other things): 'Nobody receives the gospel passively; each one as a matter of course interprets it' (Bosch 1991: 182).

Truth needs to be interpreted, otherwise it cannot be comprehended or applied. This step is essential in a dualistic view, for the 'language' of the eternal is not the same as that of the temporal. The assumption is that if one divine truth is revealed, then only one truth should find expression in this world. Clearly, however, this is not the case. As a supreme truth is interpreted and then applied, one finds not one truth being manifest, but different interpretations and applications of that which is believed to be ultimate truth.

Bosch (1991: 182) suggests that for this reason it is not appropriate to speak of 'Christian theology' but of 'Christian theologies'. This should be done without exclusively defining truth according to the parameters set by either fundamentalism or postmodernism. What Bosch is suggesting is that the recognition of the subjective nature of perceived truth according to this model is different from the perspectives held by postmodern philosophy. There is a distinct difference between the recognition of the subjective nature of perceived truth due to contextual limitations and the universal acceptance of all expressions of truth as truth. This is mainly due to the limitations imposed by the processes of interpretation and projection. The negative aspect of a dualistic approach is that it seldom acknowledges the subjective interpretation of truth and tends to slide into authoritarianism and fundamentalism. It attempts to afford individual truth a status that it should not hold – a true reflection of divine truth. It interprets individual truth as a matter of belief that does not lend itself towards either growth or conversation (Rieger 2007: 316). It is not open to criticism, and where criticism is levied, it has the freedom to merely respond with the phrase 'The truth will set you free,' implying that the respondent alone is the bearer of truth. The receiver will experience that truth and be transformed into a person who will subscribe to the same world view, philosophy and religious understanding as the respondent. Is this a feasible way of understanding salvation? Is it realistic to think that such a form of salvation will override or even erase all spheres of an individual's life that may pose a threat to such a person's experience of God?

God's truth as truth unfolding in the created order

The second perspective understands the notion of truth within the framework of the subjective nature of human interpretation and application of truth. This understanding becomes the premise from which truth is understood, engaged with and applied. Let me illustrate: imagine that we draw a line representing eternity and made a small mark representing 70 years on this line. If we believe that God – who cannot in any case be confined to or by any such line – were to reveal Godself and God's truth fully to the created realm, then a person who spends their entire life (represented by the 70 year mark) receiving and knowing God's revelation will still be left with a very small picture of God and God's truth. How can such a person even dare to claim that he or she is in possession of all the truth there is about God?

The central doctrine concerned with truth in this understanding is not soteriology as found in the previous perspective, but the doctrine of revelation. This moves the individual and community to an understanding that truth is not a static possession of the righteous, but a revealed aspect of God's being that finds dynamic expression in the created realm while giving life. This view is much more open to growth, change and conversation. Recognising the incomplete nature of perceived truth naturally leads one down a path of depending on continued revelation. It is possible for God to continue speaking to the individual or the community, despite the influences of context, culture and world view.

Once again, some questions can be asked. If God's truth is continually being revealed, how can we in the created order sift through history, philosophy, science, anthropology and the like and discover a nugget of truth, which may only be relevant for a limited time? What are the tools we use in order to take a discovered truth and use it as a basis for defining future truths still to be revealed? This perspective too can claim 'the truth will set you free', but it means something different from the previous perspective. Here it suggests that complete truth will always evade the seeker, and therefore the best that can be hoped for is that the individual will experience moments of freedom as truth is revealed.

I doubt whether the vast majority of Christians subscribe exclusively to either of these ways of looking at things. There is a natural tension between these two perspectives which means that any expression of faith is likely to tend more towards one than the other. Exclusive practice of either of these approaches is subject to too many loopholes, which in itself demonstrates the notion that complete truth cannot be found in either. But the church is still in the business of proclaiming a 'truth'; the truth of its faith. It calls this Evangelism and throughout history it has been described as being exercised through a practice called 'mission'.

MISSION AS THE PROCLAMATION OF TRUTH

> Mission has its origin neither in the official Church nor in special groups within the Church. It has its origin in God. God is a missionary God, a God who crosses frontiers towards the world ... Mission is God giving up himself, his becoming man, his laying aside of his divine prerogatives and taking our humanity, his moving into the world, in his Son and Spirit. (Bosch 1980: 239)

The church's missionary activity concerns the proclamation of truth as revealed by God. The *Good News* is the testimony of God's self-revelation and the impact it has on the world. The response to God's self-disclosure is a response of faith. Those who respond to God's revelation by faith form a community that is called the Church. The Church engages with different entities, whether institutions, communities or individuals, on the basis of God's self-revelation. Mission cannot belong to the church, for the church does not proclaim *its* discovery of the truth, but God's truth revealed and the possibility of responding to this truth by faith, as enabled by the Spirit.

The manner in which the Church proclaims this message will determine whether the recipients of the message will hear God speaking to them or not. Where the Church takes a deontologically moral stance, projecting a message that it is the sole custodian and owner of truth, the Church's message stands a very small chance of being received positively. Mission is concerned with reconciliation — reconciliation between people and reconciliation between God and creation, but 'reconciliation is only in the vocabulary of those who can afford it. It is non-existent to a person whose self-respect has been stripped away and poverty is a festering wound that consumes his soul' (Villa-Vicencio and Verwoerd 2000: 207).

If the Church proclaims its missional gospel in this way, then it cannot represent the truth, for, instead of freedom, it brings a message which imprisons people with the chains of guilt and fear. On the other hand, to speak of the way of the Kingdom is to have a very clear and definite understanding of the Church's authority to represent a way of truth and justice which can hold its own in a world which usually expects the Church's proclamation to be subjective and which lacks such assumed authority. The temptation for the Church is to comply with this inadequate expectation:

> There is a tendency among Christians to content themselves with limited goals and moderate expectations ... Our missionary enterprises will, after all, be only partly successful. Not all people will accept the gospel. Not all evil, injustice and exploitation will be removed. We should therefore – so the argument goes – not be aiming at the stars or dream of utopias but rather settle for compromises (Bosch 1980: 244).

The Church thereby finds itself in a catch-22 situation. If it represents truth as if it were its owner, it comes at the cost of freedom and reconciliation. If it offers truth from the perspective that it holds very little authority, its message is deemed to have little credibility. So how is the Church's proclamation tested? It was Albert Outler (1964) who described John Wesley's quadrilateral (Scripture, Tradition, Reason and Experience) as a measure for the attaining of truth. None of these elements was to be seen as the sole revealer of truth, but each was a pointer to truth.

DAVID BOSCH'S NOTION OF MISSION

The reader may have noticed that I have referred to David Bosch on several occasions. Bosch, in my view, gives a very good description of church mission and its claim to truth. Bosch describes three models of church mission, two of which relate directly to our understanding of truth thus far, and then offers a model that holds the church in a delicate tension between the two.

Evangelical model of mission

The first model assumes the following premise: 'if we do not do mission work, the people who have not heard the gospel will perish eternally' (Bosch 1980: 31). Surely this must be the reason for Jesus commanding the disciples to spend their time in proclaiming the gospel! As discussed earlier (see *God's truth as ultimate truth, fully imparted*), this model is based on a dualistic world view with the understanding that the truth represented by the gospel is essentially soteriological. This world is evil and destined for judgement, while the spiritual is the realm of that which is good and Godly. The Church is seen as God's instrument of salvation. Although the Church itself cannot effect salvation, it is God's instrument of salvation.

If the Church is indeed the manifestation and the holder of truth within the created realm, and this realm is the dwelling place of evil, then it is the Church's duty in mission to invade the world for the sake of its redemption. This notion is well described by Hans-Ruedi Weber (1963: 8–13). This perspective needs to answer the question whether it presents Christ as Lord of the Church only and not of the world also (Bosch 1980: 202).

Ecumenical model of mission

The second model seeks 'to overcome all the dualisms of the previous view, for instance those between eternal and temporal, soul and body, individual and community, religion and culture, evangelisation and social involvement, vertical and horizontal, salvation and liberation, proclamation and presence, religious and secular, Church and world' (Bosch 1980: 35).

As mentioned earlier (see *God's truth as truth unfolding in the created order*), this model may fall into the trap of offering a truth that is so diluted by its efforts to break away from dualism that the world does not recognise it as a message of integrity.

Emancipated Gospel

The third model offers a position which holds the previous approaches in tension. It would be wrong to assume that truth should be understood as something that renders the previous two models of mission as mutually exclusive. It is summed up in the following sentence: 'The Kingdom comes wherever Christ overcomes evil' (Bosch 1980: 209). This suggests to me that the Church's mission and its truth concerns two issues: grace and justice.

It proclaims a grace which demands justice. The truth of the gospel is not visible on the surface of our existence, because it is suppressed by the truths proposed by our culture, environment and world view (Rieger 2007: 317). To *find* the truth of the gospel is a futile exercise. God's truth is not found or discovered, for if it were, God would be dispossessed of the truth and it would belong to the finder or discoverer. The truth of the gospel is revealed differently. It is not revealed in dribs and drabs, but is revealed fully in the life and teaching of Jesus Christ. Furthermore, it is revealed through Scripture, which points to the revelation of God in Jesus Christ. Here it must be said that a distinction needs to be made between the understanding of Scripture *being* the truth and Scripture *pointing* to the truth. Where Scripture is regarded as *the* truth, as is done in literalist–fundamentalist circles, one does not find freedom, for it is a truth which binds by the letter. This is exactly the struggle between Jesus and the teachers of the law. Where Scripture is used with the understanding that it points to the truth – to God's covenant with creation, Israel, the church and the world – a truth is manifested which breaks the shackles of oppressive religion and sets people free. Let us take a look at what Anselm describes: God reveals Godself to a world which is bound by the limitations of finitude. God's existence does not depend on creation's ability to recognise God's being (Anselm 1960: 145). From this perspective all creation's perceptions of truth must be described as relative (Anselm 1960: 179). Creation's truth cannot be ultimate or absolute truth. The only absolute truth which exists is the being of God whose existence is not dependant on the limitations of finitude, but which transcends the boundaries of time and space. When God's self-revelation takes place in the realm of the created order, creation is confronted with the presence of truth in its midst. To borrow a phrase from Barth, this is an 'impossible possibility', but becomes a reality in the Incarnation: 'Only in conjunction with the revelation of absolute truth can all the relative truths of creation be known and recognised. As all things depend in their being on the being of God, so their truth and knowability depends on his truth' (Von Balthasar 1992: 144).

The tension between the ownership and the 'discovery' of truth is manifest in the tension between the divinity and humanity of Christ. Christ brings the divine truth into the realm of creation, but reveals it in such a way that it does not come across as authoritarian, but on countless occasions brings life and dignity to those who were deemed to be the least receptive to what was perceived to be God's truth.

CONCLUSION

Truth is not owned, yet it is not defined in a process. We started the conversation with the illustration of the protest banner quoting John 8: 32. This quotation is in fact misleading for it does not accurately convey what Jesus was communicating. The full verse reads 'If you make my word your home you will indeed be my disciples; you will come to know the truth, and the truth will set you free.' (John 8: 31-32, *New Jerusalem Bible*). Otherwise stated 'If you abide by what I say, more and more you will understand the truth, and the truth will set you free.' (Buttrick 1952: 601).

Truth is about both soteriology and revelation. The truth should set us free continually. If at any point the church or the Christian maintains that they have attained the truth in full, then the truth has ceased to be present in their midst. If the truth were claimed to have been discovered, then it falls prey to subjective scepticism. Truth to the Christian is the journey to become Christ-like, thus transforming the Christian from a believer into a disciple.

BIBLIOGRAPHY

Anselm 1960. *Anselm: Fides quaerens intellectum.* London: SCM Press

Bosch, D J 1980. *Witness to the world: The Christian Mission in Theological perspective.* London: Marshall, Morgan & Scott.

Bosch, D J 1991. *Transforming mission: Paradigm shifts in Theology of Mission.* New York: Orbis Books.

Burden, J J and Prinsloo, W S (eds) 1987. *Dialogue with God: The literature of the Old Testament.* Volume 3. Cape Town: Tafelberg Publishers.

Buttrick, G A (ed) 1952. *The Interpreter's Bible.* Volume VIII. Nashville: Abingdon Press.

Kümmel, W G 1970. *Introduction to the New Testament.* London: SCM Press.

Outler, A C (ed) 1964. *John Wesley: A library of Protestant thought.* New York: Oxford University Press.

Rieger, J 2007. *Christ and Empire: From Paul to Postcolonial times.* Minneapolis: Fortress Press.

The New Jerusalem Bible 1990. London: Darton, Longman & Todd.

Villa-Vicencio, C and Verwoerd, W (eds) 2000. *Looking back, Reaching forward: Reflections on the Truth and Reconciliation Commission of South Africa.* Cape Town: Cape Town University Press.

Von Balthasar, H U 1992. *The Theology of Karl Barth.* Translated by E T Oakes. San Francisco: Ignatius Press.

Weber, H R 1963. *Salty Christians.* New York: The Seabury Press.

WHY YOU CAN'T SIMPLY TRUST EVERYTHING YOU READ

Dion Forster

Spirituality, postmodernism and the interpretation of Scripture – reading the same Bible and reaching differing conclusions.

1. INTRODUCTION: WHY YOU CAN'T SIMPLY TRUST EVERYTHING YOU READ (OR SEE)!

Have you ever wondered how it is possible that people who read the same Bible and lovingly serve the same Lord, can reach such different (and even conflicting) conclusions on matters such as abortion or homosexuality?

For some years I have served as a member of the Methodist Church of Southern Africa's (MCSA) Doctrine, Ethics, and Worship Commission (DEWCOM). DEWCOM is the committee of the Church that is charged with researching and considering doctrinal and ethical issues on behalf of the Church. At times the committee offers guidance to the Conference of the MCSA. In doing so the aim is to help the Church to formulate an official position on a particular matter. DEWCOM frequently has to gather information about the various theological positions that Methodists hold on particular issues, interpret those positions, and then suggest why one position may be more Christian and responsible to hold than another. This is a tricky business! In a Church as large and diverse as ours there are frequently different, and at times even conflicted, positions on doctrinal and ethical matters. In the years that I have served on the committee we have considered various topics. Perhaps the most controversial of these has been the committee's work on the Christian response to abortion, and the work that was done to guide the Church in deciding how to relate to persons with a same-sex (homosexual) orientation.

In 2004 I presented a paper at the 10th anniversary celebrations of John Wesley College Kilnerton (then the seminary of the MCSA)[2]. The central argument of this paper was as follows: a study of the feedback from the DEWCOM same-sex discussion document indicated that most persons cited their interpretation of the Bible as the most influential element in forming their theological and ethical position about persons with a same-sex orientation. Most respondents suggested that their view was formed by the following sources, in order of priority: the Bible first, then natural theology (i.e. that we are created as men and women), and finally social and cultural values. This priority of sources was found both among persons who felt that a same-sex orientation was incompatible with the Christian faith, *and* among those who felt that persons with a same-sex orientation should be welcomed and embraced in the same manner as one would embrace heterosexual Christians. Both 'groups' quoted verses from scripture, and formulated their arguments based on their interpretation of scripture. The assumption for most respondents was that their interpretation of the scriptures was valid, and thus that their particular view was 'Biblical', whilst other views were neither Biblical nor valid. The paper I presented argued the point that the majority of positions presented had their starting point not in scripture per se, but in the 'a priori' social and contextual factors that influenced the person's interpretation of scripture. In other words, one did not have to read very deeply to see that certain texts and interpretive methods were favoured over others, and that these tended to reflect the

---

2   This paper, entitled *Christianity, inclusivity, and homosexuality: An interpretation of responses to the Methodist Church of Southern Africa's discussion document on same sex relationships,* is unpublished. Please feel free to contact me directly at http://www.dionforster.com if you would like a copy of the paper.

social and cultural values of the group concerned. Some texts were ignored, whilst the meaning and interpretation of others was 'stretched' and 'distorted' to make particular points.

This research highlighted two concerns for me: first, that most persons are ignorant of the fact that there are various social and contextual factors that significantly influence our reading and interpretation of scripture in general. These factors can be likened to 'coloured' lenses in a pair of reading glasses. If you have red coloured reading glasses, everything you look at will have a red tinge. One can become so used to this 'perspective' that you forget that there are other colours, and that everything you see is not red, but that it is merely your perspective of it that makes it appear red! Sadly, when this happens we tend to be intolerant of the positions of others since we judge them without understanding our own bias. Second, I came to realise that since most people are unaware of their own bias, they are seldom tolerant and sensitive to the unconscious biases of others. If we understood that all of us struggle with a biased interpretation we may be a little more tolerant of the views of others, and perhaps even a little more willing to engage their view, both so that we can understand it, and also so that they can understand the effect of their bias on the situation. The sad result of this lack of engagement and openness is that individuals and groups can fall into the trap of assuming that only their interpretation is correct. Moreover, rather than understanding how another person or group arrives at their outcome, they are simply dismissed as wrong, misguided, or even heretical.

At this stage you may doubt how powerful this 'bias' can be on your interpretation of scripture. It is quite easy to illustrate the power of unconscious and tacit bias by using a simple visual test.

Robert Laws, a Scottish missionary working in Malawi in the 1880s, discovered that the influence of culture, one's environment and context, can have a significant effect on one's visual perception and, if that is the case, such forces will also shape other points of view (such as one's interpretation of scripture). Take a look at the picture on the next page. What you see will largely depend on where you live in the world. After you have examined the picture for a few moments and noticed the elements that make up the scene, please read on for a more detailed explanation of the theory.

So what did you see in this simple picture? What is above the woman's head? Where are the people seated?

When scientists showed a similar sketch to people from East and Southern Africa, nearly all the participants in the experiment said the woman was balancing a box or metal container on her head since women commonly carry containers with water and food on their heads in those areas. In cultures that contain few angular visual cues (such as square buildings), the family is seen to be sitting under a tree. Westerners, on the other hand, are accustomed to the corners and box-like shapes of contemporary architecture and so they are more likely to place the family indoors and to interpret the rectangle above the woman's head as a window through which shrubbery can be seen. Remarkable, isn't it?

Can you see how one's context and culture can shape and inform different interpretations of the same picture? People from different places and with different life experiences look at the same picture and see vastly different things. If this is the case with a fairly recent artwork, one can only imagine how complex understanding the differences in the interpretation of Biblical texts among people from Africa, Asia, Europe, and the Americas could be! Culture, context, and of course one's faith, are all significant influences in our use and interpretation of scripture.

In this chapter we shall discuss the relationship between spirituality, postmodernism, and our interpretation of scripture. I hoped that as you gain a fuller understanding of the concepts of Christian spirituality and the complexity of the influences of postmodern thought on your faith, that you will gain some insight into the elements that shape and inform your own reading of scripture, and the views of others who may or may not agree with you. In the end, my hope is that this will allow you to be more tolerant and respectful of the views and perspectives of others.

2. SPIRITUALITY AND YOUR STORY

Why is spirituality so important in interpreting the Bible? Well, spirituality is that element of our faith that is most 'real' and tangible – it is a term that is meant to express the experience of loving God and living out that love in all of one's daily life. Spirituality involves both sacred activities, such as prayer and worship, and secular activities, such as acts of service and one's daily work. In short, one could conclude that spirituality is a lived discipline. It takes place within a particular socio-historical context and as such there is a close link between spirituality, the elements that compose it, and the context within which it is formed. Within this context Kristo notes that spirituality

> ... is part of a story, and it should be considered as such if one wants to get to the bottom of the nature of mystical experience ... It cannot be sufficiently emphasised that the mystical journey is a response to a definite, specific horizon. (Kristo in Eire 1990: 59).

Culture, tradition, social and political surroundings, as well as sacred texts and faith communities, are all factors that influence the development and practice of spirituality. By the same token spirituality also acts on culture, tradition, the use of sacred sources (such as the Bible) and the experience and participation of individuals and groups in society. One could conclude that spirituality and culture are mutually transformative in nature. Spirituality and culture act upon one another in order to bring about a constant cycle of change and growth. Hence, in order to understand how your perspective and experience of God and God's power and will in your life influence your reading and interpretation of the Bible, it is necessary to investigate dominant social and religious trends in your context (and the contexts of others). Understanding these trends will help you to understand your own spirituality, and the spirituality of others, in turn giving you an insight into the influence that these approaches to God and life have upon the formulation of faith and theology.

In the sections below we shall consider one of the most significant social and philosophical forces of our time, postmodernism. Postmodernism will be defined and related to an understanding of spirituality. I deliberately use the term 'an understanding of spirituality' since you shall soon see that speaking of a single spirituality can be a minefield! Spirituality is as complex as postmodernity! However, this chapter will characterise an understanding of spirituality by listing some of its constitutive elements that are widely accepted by theologians. Having presented the concepts of postmodernism and spirituality, there will be a discussion on the manner in which these two relate to one another within the context of our use of scripture. This chapter also considers some benefits and pitfalls that arise from a biblical spirituality that operates within the postmodernist paradigm. Finally we shall discuss some examples of postmodernist hermeneutics that are able to inform and enrich contemporary spirituality and help us to approach the interpretation of scripture with integrity and respect.

3. TOWARDS A DEFINITION OF SPIRITUALITY

An essential component in understanding the relationship between spirituality, postmodernism and scripture, necessitates a grasp of the constituent elements. Whilst there are no exacting definitions for spirituality, one is able to indicate, in a broad sense at least, some characteristic elements within the study and practice of spirituality in the academy and the Church (cf.

Eire 1990: 53). In the section that follows, three aspects will be mentioned that are common to most contemporary definitions of spirituality (cf. Schneiders 1989: 687–692; Cousins 1990: 41).

Some scholars have expressed a measure of frustration at their inability to 'pin down' this 'nebulous phenomenon known as spirituality' (Eire 1990: 53). What makes a definition of spirituality so difficult to 'pin down' is the fact that it seems to cover everything from mystical devotion to social action and a myriad of disciplines, activities, and realities in between. It would seem that the subject has no boundaries, seeking to encompass various 'truths' and experiences (it is interesting to note that this is a central characteristic of the postmodern paradigm).

This section will, however, present a few necessary elements in the study and practice of spirituality that could help in our task of understanding it. Please take note that these are not conclusive suggestions. The postmodern perspective on 'truth' is that it is no more possible to completely define truth than it is to play a piece of music that would render all other music obsolete! Rather, each attempt at expressing truth adds insight, depth, and richness. The points I shall mention below will merely serve to facilitate the purpose of this chapter, which is to discuss the relationship between spirituality, the Bible and postmodernism.

You may ask why it is even necessary to attempt to define spirituality if it truly is such a nebulous and difficult task. Sheldrake notes that if one were completely unable to define, articulate, and to some extent at least objectify spirituality, then it would mean that it is completely incomprehensible and thus nonsensical. Hence he concludes that if spirituality has 'no conceptual limits, effectively it means nothing' (Sheldrake 1991: 40). Thus I wish to suggest these 'conceptual' guidelines within which I believe spirituality functions and can, to some extent, be articulated.

First, most theologians would agree that spirituality, at some level at least, has to do with one's experience. By this I mean that there needs to be a locus within which spirituality takes place, and that this locus is the human person. True spirituality is mediated through the person's very existence; his or her senses, emotions and needs. In most cases these experiences are experiences of transcendence, that is, they facilitate contact with a God who transcends one's reality, and is instrumental in the shifting of one's boundaries.

An effective spirituality will frequently challenge one's worldview; deepening one's experience of a relationship with God, the self and others.

Second, most theologians agree that spiritual experiences are experiences that have a cognitive element to them. Eire asks the question:

> If, as Cousins and many others assert, there is an ultimate reality to be experienced, how do human beings perceive and describe this reality? (1990: 58)

Perception is an important element in making sense of our experiences. Since Descartes coined the remarkable insight *cogito ergo sum* (I think therefore I am), cognition has become an essential element of affirming and articulating our experience of reality. Thus, I would suggest that spirituality is that state, emotion or experience where the individual or group comes to know and understand something of the fundamental and ultimate truth of their existence. That is why questions such as the one by St Francis of Assisi are so important: 'My God! My God! What are you? Who am I?' Such questions seem to express the notion of the importance of the cognitive element of spirituality. At some level we all long to understand who God is, who we are, and what is meaning and intention of our life here on earth is. However, it needs to be said that cognition should not be rigidly equated with reason. I would assert that one is able have experiences which are inexplicable yet cognitive. A feeling of love for a spouse or child is one such experience. One feels it, one can describe it (to some extent), one knows that one loves this person – yet one cannot fully explain what this love is. Of course there are many wonderful examples of such experiences in the lives of Christians throughout the ages. I have found the writings of the continental mystics, and the 'autotheists', such as Meister Eckhard, particularly expressive of this notion.

Third, I would suggest that spirituality falls within the domain of history and the sciences as much as it falls into the domain of theology and religion. The reasons for this will become clearer later in this chapter as an understanding of the postmodern paradigm is considered. What is important at this point, however, is the assertion that the link between the Christian faith and history is not incidental (cf. Forster 2007: 31–34). Jesus enters human history at a particular point, and this is in keeping with God's will. If one accepts that history is important in the Christian faith then it means that spirituality (our experience and expression of our love for God) is also historically located. It is connected to persons, events, and places. As such, one can conclude that spirituality is not a complete mystery, as some have asserted. There are aspects of spirituality that are explicable and can be shared with others. This does not mean that everyone will have the same spiritual experiences, or even that persons who share a common spiritual experience will express it in the same manner and form. Rather it asserts that spirituality can be articulated, shared and developed by making use of the tools of language, symbol and philosophy. In this sense then, spirituality is both a single discipline and mutli-disciplinary. As Eire notes:

> because the study of spirituality is focussed on experiences ... it continually needs to be refreshed by contact with that environment ... [along with this] established academic disciplines and the study of spirituality will best coexist and promote each other's well being when their investigations share a common sense of order and direction. (1990: 61)

In conclusion, spirituality is 'a fundamental dimension of human being, the lived experience which actualises that dimension, and the academic discipline which studies that experience' (Schneiders 1989: 678). As such one could quite safely assume that spirituality is not a prescriptive discipline, but rather a descriptive discovery. Spirituality seeks not so much to prescribe, although some have tried to do this, but rather to describe existential reality in relation to God, others, and oneself.

Since spirituality is existential (i.e. experienced in the contextual existence of individuals and communities) and contextual (i.e. formed by culture, geography, history and sociology) it can be understood to some extent. This understanding can help one to deconstruct many elements of one's own theology and faith – elements that will have a significant effect on how one reads and interprets the Bible.

4. NOSTALGIA AND THE UNKNOWN: MODERNISM AND POSTMODERNISM CONSIDERED

It must be noted that the term 'postmodernism' is somewhat elastic and nomadic. By this I mean that it stretches over many disciplines and frequently moves from one meaning to another. On the one hand it has been used to describe particular artists, styles and buildings; on the other hand it has claimed to describe the whole contemporary period of advanced consumer society 'by naming either its dominant socio-economic trends or its prevailing sensibility' (Brooker and Brooker 1997: 1).

This section of the paper will discuss the terms modernism and postmodernism, seeking to extrapolate and investigate the meaning that has become attached to each of these terms within contemporary society and the academy.

a) Nostalgia – modernism considered

We begin by investigating the etymological and historical precursor to post-modernism, that is, modernism. Hunter suggests that modernism 'has always been used to set one period in time apart from another in terms of old and new' (1996: 13). As such, modernism is quite simply a term that is used to differentiate two historical periods from one another: modernism and the period that followed it, namely postmodernism.

Modernism, as a philosophical notion, has its roots in the 17th century with the increasing confidence in reason, science and technology that was associated with such thinkers as René Descartes and Isaac Newton. As an historical period, however, it only becomes entrenched through western culture in the first five or six decades of the 20th century (Lundin 1993: 3) with its extreme confidence in reason, human and scientific ability, as well as social and political developments in the West. It was the age of flight, the motor car, telecommunications, the atomic bomb, television, relativity theory and microbiology.

Hunter (1996: 13–14) suggests a number of characteristic elements of the modernist world view. He notes that modernity places a great deal of confidence and emphasis on the human person as the subjective controller of knowledge. In this regard, reason is exalted as the primary conceptual tool through which all things are sought out, investigated and categorised. The goal or *'teleos'* of knowledge is to master the positive in order to find what is useful, efficient, and true, and once that has been discovered to make use of it. As the great modernist television series, *Star Trek*, stated 'to boldly go where no man has gone before'. Thus Bell suggests that in simpler terms 'modern' persons 'concentrated on reaching for all because it is human. Man [sic] concentrates on demystifying what is thought to be within his or her realm ... to know it all, to achieve immediate knowledge of everything' (in Hunter 1996: 14). For the modernist, knowledge reigns supreme.

It was out of this paradigm that the historical critical method of biblical criticism gained popular acclaim in the early part of this century. This is a method that seeks to break the text into pieces so that in examining and understanding the constituent parts, the whole may be understood. Such a method is restrictive, prescriptive, and, according to Hunter, not consistent. Since 'those parts of the text that are viewed as not fitting the general interpretative trend or translation of the author are easily amended or seen as secondary' (1996: 19).

Within the modernist paradigm everything is explicable – people, cultures, behaviour and religion are all confined to strict rational categories. It was assumed that there are very few grey areas. Many today long for the security of such a world view, as seen in the resurgence of literalist and fundamentalist movements within the world's living faiths.

I frequently perceive deterministic modernist undertones in the narrow understandings of scripture that I, and others, apply in order to take mastery of a situation or experience. For example, many of us feel that when we find a 'proof text' to support our particular view we are vindicated from considering any other point of view. Sadly, such a perspective is misleading and incomplete. For example, just because I have discovered what role a spark plug plays in keeping a combustion motor running, it does not mean that I should not also consider the role of the fuel injector or the piston. A modernist spiritual perspective often makes the mistake of thinking that it alone is 'true' and 'correct' without considering that it is only a part of the picture of reality and truth, since, as has already been said, it is bound by particular contextual and historical factors.

b) The unknown – postmodernism considered

Postmodernism is more an evolution of thought than a revolution. It is not something completely new (if there is such a thing as 'completely new'). Rather, postmodernism, as its name suggests, is the period and associated world view that follows modernism.

Lundin suggests that postmodernism is a response to the metanarratives of rigour, characterisation, progress and development in all spheres of life, that were so characteristic of the modernist era (1993: 4). Thus postmodernism is a reaction to the rigid and narrow characterisations of modernism.

The most obvious examples of this reaction, or evolution, are to be found in playful and allusive architecture and literature, as well as music, the visual media and in the growing information technologies. Historically, it seems that the postmodern reaction began in France. In literature, it is the author Derrida who coined the term *la difference*. Hunter suggests three meanings to this term. First, it means '"to differ" – to be unlike or dissimilar in nature, quality or form'. Second, it relates to the Latin word *differe* – meaning 'to scatter, disperse'. Finally, it carries the meaning '"to defer" – to delay, postpone' (1996: 25). Derrida's phrase and the meanings that come from it sum up to a large extent the ethos of the postmodern paradigm – to be different, to disperse and delay.

Postmodernism, as is the case with spirituality, is a somewhat elusive concept, defying a single definition (cf. Hunter 1996: 15). Definitions, by nature, tend to draw objects, thoughts and groups together. Postmodernism by its very nature seeks to allow for a plurality of meanings, breaking down monist and restrictive characterisations in favour of diversity and difference. It encourages a measure of relativism and rejects the notion of one underlying, all-encompassing truth:

> Postmodernism does not wish to be the thread that binds a number of elements of our era together. It does not want to be

the underlying philosophy … This would undermine the character of postmodernism as pluralistic, allowing for all possible meanings, opinions and trends. (Hunter 1996: 15)

One of the characteristic trends of postmodernism that is of particular interest to this paper is its suspicion of the modern person. In particular, postmodernism is suspicious of the picture of humanity that was given in modernity i.e. that of an all-powerful entity that is capable of knowing all things, objectively able to observe and reason his or her way through all situations of life. In the postmodern paradigm the person is understood in relation to circumstances, whether social, economic, political or psychological (Hunter 1996: 16). The person no longer determines the facts; rather, he or she is determined by them, no longer shaping meaning, but a result of the shaping process: 'As such man [sic] has no critical self but for the self given him by his circumstances' (Hunter 1996: 16).

I'm certain that many readers will hear alarm bells sounding in their heads at this point! Surely for the Christian there must be some fundamental truth that transcends the individual's context and circumstances? Surely one cannot simply be shaped by each passing 'wind of doctrine' and experience? Brian McLaren would argue that postmodernism is not *less* rigorous about the truth in merely saying that all truths are correct. Rather, he argues that the postmodernist mindset has to be *more* rigorous in its discovery of truth since it must question *all* truths (even those which have long been held to be unquestionable) (cf. McLaren 2004: 13ff).

Franke comments on this new 'questioning' disposition, noting that the theological certainties of previous ages are changing: 'strange things are happening in unexpected places, long-familiar assumptions are being called into question' (in McLaren 2004: 13).

In relation to biblical studies, this opens up a whole new world of possibility! The understanding of God's capacity to reveal God's will and love is no longer bound to fit into the narrow confines of tradition and history. Rather, God is free once again to simply speak! There is a realisation that since God is speaking to persons, persons who are in particular social and historical contexts, there is a strong likelihood that there will be some variety and difference in what is revealed and received. It is important to note that the reader now enters into the hermeneutic process. Since his or her life is important to God, and God is likely to want to address him or her, God will do so within the situation in which the individual or community exists. This is the joy of the influence of postmodernism. However, there is also a great danger in this! Many have assumed that because there are so many 'truths' that all truths hold equal weight and validity. This is simply a mistake. There does need to be an equally stringent suspicion of what the reader brings to the text in the postmodernist approach to the interpretation of scripture. Just as the modernist brings a bias and a framework to the reading of the text, so too does the postmodernist.

In the breakdown of the subject/object dichotomy comes a process of mutual transformation. As the reader is transformed by the text, the meaning of the text itself is transformed by the one who reads it. In this approach to scripture there is a far greater openness to new discovery and growth. Yet there is a great danger in wandering from orthodoxy and the traditions of the faith.

5. POSTMODERNISM AND SPIRITUALITY

At the start of this chapter, the assertion was made that culture and context affect spirituality. Spirituality in turn influences and informs one's reading of scripture. It has already been argued that authentic spirituality takes place within the locus of the person, and as such is expressed and experienced through the social and cultural trappings which surround him or her. In this regard, it is vital that one gains an understanding of how spirituality and postmodernism act upon each other and function together, and how this in turn affects the reading of scripture.

If modernism asserts absolute individualism, the subject over against an objective reality, then postmodernism asserts relations and interdependence, a lack of distinction between subject and object. Contemporary spirituality shares these elements with the postmodern paradigm. The clearest expressions of such views come from recent discoveries in the areas of the natural and human sciences. Sharpe, a quantum-physicist, writes:

> No human act, no element of life or the environment, no human activity is an island, any more than the individual is an island. (Sharpe 1990: 114)

As in postmodernism, contemporary spirituality affirms that a person's context, family, and geographical and social location are constitutive of a person's identity. In this regard, there is always a certain amount of suspicion of the baggage that a person brings along with him or her when articulating and interpreting experiences and reality. This is particularly so when it comes to the biblical text.

Moreover, there is in contemporary spirituality and postmodernism a notion of interconnected wholeness. In its most basic form, this belief maintains that there is some form of interconnectivity, solidarity and mutual interdependence between all persons and the created order (some would go so far as to include God in the relational dependence). In this regard, the quantum-physicist Schrödinger writes:

> Inconceivable as it seems to ordinary reason, you – and all other conscious beings as such – are all in all. Hence this life of yours you are living is not merely a piece of the entire existence, but it is in a certain sense the *whole* ... Thus you can throw yourself flat on the ground, stretched out upon Mother Earth, with the certain conviction that you are one with her and she with you. (Schrödinger in Wilber 1975: 108)

Such understandings have become increasingly popular in the West, and have been the accepted norm in eastern spiritualities for centuries. The modernist's desire to overcome, to control and to possess is replaced by a desire for peaceful co-existence, a realisation of the fragility of our planet's ecosystem, and the need to live in interdependence with other persons and all of creation. The destructive power of war, greed, and capitalist gain have been so damagingly displayed in recent world history – perhaps the war in Iraq is a most poignant example of the worst of humanity's nature. One of the most famous scientists of our time, summed up this feeling as follows: 'A human [may experience] ... himself, his thoughts and feelings as something separated from the rest – a kind of optical delusion of his consciousness. This delusion is a kind of prison for us ... Our task must be to free ourselves from this prison.' (Einstein in Wilber 1991: 18)

In a very real sense, contemporary spirituality has developed out of, and alongside, contemporary culture. It is the developments and discoveries of modern society that, to a large extent, have shaped contemporary spirituality. However, this movement is not only in one direction. Spirituality is pervading modern society, with more and more persons striving for transcendence beyond mere material reality. In this regard, spirituality serves as an important corrective to certain dangerous elements of the postmodernist paradigm, e.g. relativism and individualism. Post-modern spirituality refocuses the power to make decisions, to govern and to guide in the hands of communities. Truth is no longer the weapon of the individual, but one of the riches of the community. De Villiers comments on truth saying that it 'is an agreement reached within a community of believers as to what forms the basis of their understanding' (1991: 150).

6. TEXT AND CONTEXT: CONTEMPORARY SPIRITUALITY AND BIBLICAL INTERPRETATION

Having discussed postmodernism and spirituality – some of their characteristic elements as well as their influences – we will now move on to consider the effect that postmodernism has on the interpretation of the scriptures.

One of the most vividly evident aspects of postmodernism in contemporary interpretative methods is postmodernism's desire to challenge traditional interpretations of the Biblical text. Whereas the modern period placed a great deal of emphasis on textual criticism, the postmodern period moves beyond such a strict dichotomy between the text and the reader. Hence, in a postmodern reading of scripture, interpretation is dependant upon both textual *and* self criticism, that is, text and context.

De Villiers expresses this thought clearly in saying that the 'reader response' method of biblical interpretation (which is itself a thoroughgoing postmodernist method) 'rejects the naïve realist position of interpretation and accepts that the reader is actively involved in the creation of meaning in Biblical scholarship'. Furthermore, he notes that this shows clearly 'how close many scholars are to some basic tenets of postmodernism' (1991: 149).

Such a method has a tremendously positive effect on both scholarship and the development of spirituality, not to mention that it creates greater understanding and harmony in diverse Christian communities. It serves as an important corrective to the modernist methods of interpretation that, although they were rigorous and precise in attempting to draw meaning out of the text, failed to recognise the tremendous part that the interpreter plays in the hermeneutic process. The interpreter, in a modernist sense, was assumed to be completely objective and free of bias. The reality is that the interpreter always influences the reading of the text. His or her theology, life experience, previous contact with the text, and faith community all feed into what ultimately arises from the text.

Thus, context is of the utmost importance. However, it is not only the context of the reader that is important, but also that of the author, the audience and any redactors of the text (cf. Lundin, Thiselton and Walhout's discussion of Baird 1985: 90 ff.). De Villiers uses the example of Breech to show how modernist readings of scripture often fell into the trap of removing the text from its context and transposing it into the context of the interpreter (cf. De Villiers 1991: 153–154). I have witnessed this mistake particularly in relation to the same-sex discussion. Many interpreters have simply assumed that references in the Bible to sexual interaction between persons of the same sex can be directly related to contemporary consenting, loving relationships between adults of the same gender. This is certainly not an accurate assumption since most of the texts in the Old and New Testaments that address sexual contact between persons of the same gender are addressing issues of sexual abuse, lust, or impure religious practises.[3]

Questions that need to be considered in a postmodern reading of the text include, amongst others, the following: Who is the author? What is the author's context? Who is the audience? What is the purpose of the text? In what situation do the audience find themselves? What is the author trying to convey from his or her context to that of the audience?

---

3   For a superb discussion on these texts please see Rev Dr Walter Wink's unpublished article entitled *Homosexuality and the Bible* – it can be found at http://www.soulforce.org/article/homosexuality-bible-walter-wink

Some of these questions may look familiar, since they correspond quite closely to the historical-critical method. However, where a postmodernist reading of scripture goes further is that it attempts to investigate two further histories within the interpretative process. These are the history and context of the redactor as well as the history and context of the reader. So this approach will ask: Who is the reader? What informs the reader's understanding of the text? With what questions is the reader approaching the text? These will be discussed in more detail below.

In terms of redaction, it is commonly accepted that many biblical texts were edited and changed, for whatever reasons, before being put together in the form in which we find them today. An investigation of what was left out and why it was changed, is just as important as the investigation of what was retained and for what reasons it was retained. A similar revolution has taken place within the study of history, in what Sheldrake calls a study of the underside of history (cf. 1995: 31 ff.). Hence, if one is able to gain some understanding of the redactor, his or her history, as well as his or her intent in including certain sections of the text whilst omitting others, one will gain a clearer picture of the meaning and intent of a text. Nonetheless, even questions such as these are nothing new, since they fit into the ambit of form criticism.

As mentioned above, postmodernism has its most pronounced effect on hermeneutics by focusing on the role of the reader within the interpretative process. Thus, one is not only critical of the text, its history and form, one is also critical of oneself.

It is in this regard that the most radical outcomes of a postmodernist reading of scripture can be seen. If one asserts that the history and context of the reader affects the meaning of the text, then one needs to accept that the text itself does not contain all the inherent value to constitute 'absolute truth'. Stated more simply, such a reading of scripture would imply that there is no single absolutely truthful interpretation of the text. Each text can have more than one reading that contains elements of the truth or, more precisely, perspectives on the truth. It is in this area that deconstructionist readings of the text have made a great contribution.

The deconstructionist method of biblical studies examines the link between words and that to which they refer (i.e. the signifier and the signified) (cf. Adam 1995: 28). The West has become captive to what Derrida calls 'logocentrism' (Lundin, Thiselton & Walhout 1985: 34). By 'logocentrism' Derrida suggests that the West has become caught up in a mistaken metaphysics, understanding notions such as reality, truth and virtue in terms of the accepted meaning we attach to the words used to describe such concepts. For Derrida, reality takes shape for persons through our words (Lundin, Thiselton & Walhout 1985: 34). Thus, language is not grounded in metaphysical certainty; words are creative, they do not contain absolute, intrinsic meaning – such meaning is created through context and association. The question posed by deconstructionists is: How do we know? How do I know what a person intends me to understand, for example, when they refer to a 'Mercedes'? This could be a make of car, but it could just as well be the name of a person! The word only takes on meaning within its context. So Adam suggests that by 'posing the how-do-we-know question, deconstruction displaces the logos from its position of authority' (1995: 28). Hence, a text is no longer bound to one absolute meaning. Derrida's *la différence* denotes that there can never be one absolute meaning for a text that will overarch all others, just as there could never be one absolute piece of music to end all symphonies. Meaning will change as text and context interact with each other.

Such an understanding of scripture is of great value, particularly in a pastoral setting, since it allows that no one view of scripture is necessarily of greater truth than any other. Within the modernist paradigm great divisions arose between the highly skilled and educated elite, and a less skilled and less educated mass. Interpretation and truth were weapons of the elite. Now there is a realisation that academic, pastoral and devotional applications of the text are of equal value and importance, each serving a valuable function within its own context.

The final aspect of postmodernism and contemporary spirituality and their approach to scripture that I would like to raise is the notion of intertextuality. As mentioned above interconnectedness and mutual dependence are clear traits in both postmodernism and contemporary spirituality. As such they have had an influence on biblical scholarship. Intertextuality affirms that each portion of the overall text forms an integral part of the whole. It is now widely accepted that most biblical writers made use of portions of the scriptures that were available to them when writing their books. Hunter notes that intertextuality not only influenced the creation of the text, but that it also influences its reading (Hunter 1996: 27), affirming once again that the context and theology of the reader form part of the suppositions with which he or she approaches the text. Thus, intertextuality has effects beyond the studied text, reaching into the context of the reader, what he or she has read, and how it has shaped and moulded the reader's life and spirituality.

7. SOME CONCLUSIONS

Whilst postmodernism has had many negative effects on western society and culture, it has also had many positive influences. Most notably, perhaps, is that it has given rise to what Sheldrake has called 'postmaterialism' (1995: 4). There has been a rediscovery of notions such as spirituality and community among ordinary Christians and in everyday life. Such positive advances in popular culture have a tremendous effect upon the spiritual climate of the world's nations, filtering into all spheres of life, and as such they have effected some radical changes in biblical studies as well. Models such as the 'reader response' method have created an opportunity to understand that the reader brings as much to the meaning of texts as the texts themselves. The process of discovering and making meaning within and with scripture is fundamentally framed by the world in which we live. This rediscovery has not only allowed for new discoveries and insights in theology, but has also led to a rigorous and careful consideration of the influence that the reader's context has upon their understanding of the text.

In short, one could conclude that because Christianity is a lived relationship that starts within the individual believer and finds its deepest and truest meaning within the faithful community, there is a far greater need to measure one's own beliefs against the beliefs of others. My interpretation of a passage from the Bible, and my view of a particular social or ethical issue, needs to be considered in the light of the other views and positions I encounter within the Christian community. At times it will be necessary to hold views that may seem contradictory, in a dynamic tension of loving unity in order to move closer to the truth. After all, is this not what God does in loving a sinful humanity? Our imperfection, when held in tension with God's perfection, is the most vivid illustration of God's grace and love. Similarly, I may find that my reading of the Bible, when held in tension with an alternate reading of the same text, may give new insights and fresh revelations, and may bring both myself, and others, closer to the truth.

In conclusion, I would like to encourage Methodists to treat one another's theological, religious and cultural convictions with respect and dignity. Whilst there may be some issues upon which we struggle to agree, there are many stronger truths that will always bind us together.

SELECT BIBLIOGRAPHY

Adam, A K M 1995. *What is post-modern biblical criticism?* Minneapolis: Fortress press.

Brooker P, Brooker W (eds) 1997. *Post-modern after – images: A reader in film television and video.* New York: Arnold.

Cousins, E H 1990. What is Christian spirituality? *Modern Christian spirituality.* (Ed. Hanson, B) pp.39-44. Atlanta: Scholars press.

De Villiers, P G R 1991. The end of hermeneutics? One New Testament studies and post-modernism. *Neotestamentica* 25 (1), 145–156.

Eire, C M N 1990. Major problems in the definition of spirituality as an academic discipline. *Modern Christian spirituality.* (Ed. Hanson, B) pp.53–64. Atlanta: Scholars Press.

Forster, D A 2001. *Wesleyan Spirituality: An introduction.* Cape Town. Methodist Publishing House.

Forster, D A 2004. *Christianity, inclusivity and homosexuality: An interpretation of responses to the same sex discussion document of DEWCOM.* Unpublished paper presented at the John Wesley College Kilnerton 10th anniversary celebrations.

Forster, D A 2007. *Christ at the centre – Discovering the Cosmic Christ in the spirituality of Dom Bede Griffiths.* Kempton Park. AcadSA Publishers.

Forster, D A 2008a. *An uncommon spiritual path – finding Jesus beyond conventional Christianity.* Kempton Park. AcadSA Publishers.

Forster, D A 2008b. *Methodism in Southern Africa – a celebration of Wesleyan Mission.* Cape Town, Kempton Park. AcadSA Publishers (A project of the Education for Ministry and Mission Unit of the MCSA and Africa Upper Room Ministries).

Glenna, E 1992. *Postmodernism, reason and religion*. New York: Routledge.

Griffin, D R (ed) 1988. Post-modern spirituality and society. *Spirituality and society*. New York: State University of New York.

Hanson, B C (ed) 1990. *Modern Christian spirituality*. Atlanta: Scholars Press.

Hunter, J 1996. *Faces of a lamenting city*. Frankfurt: Peter Lang.

Lundin, R 1993. *The culture of interpretation: Christian faith and the post-modern world*. Michigan: William B Eerdmans Publishing.

Lundin R, Thiselton A C, and Walhout C (eds) 1985. *The responsibility of hermeneutics*. Michigan: William B. Eerdmans publishing.

McKnight, E V 1988. *Post-modern use of the Bible*. Nashville: Abingdon Press.

McLaren, B D 2004. *A Generous Orthodoxy*. Grand Rapids, MI. Zondervan.

Sharpe, K 1990. Relating the physics and religion of David Bohm. *Zygon*, 25.1, 105–122.

Sheldrake, P 1995. *Spirituality and history*. London: SPCK.

Sheldrake, R 1996. Mysticism and the new science. *The other half of my soul*. Bruteau, B (ed). Wheaton: Quest Books.

Wilber, K 1975. Psychologia perennis: The spectrum of consciousness. *Journal of transpersonal psychology*, 7.2, 105–131.

TOWARDS METAPHORS OF HEALING AND TRANSFORMATION

Vusi Vilikati

INTRODUCTION

At the heart of who we are as a Church in Southern Africa is the question of what it means to become God's agent of healing and transformation. This vision and yearning is born out of the various realities of our context. Over the last two decades our subcontinent has gone through a number of political, economic and social changes. In 1994 we celebrated South Africa's victory over the Apartheid system and soon we realised that there were new challenges that emerged with democracy. We have witnessed the humiliation of countries like Zimbabwe and Mozambique by political and natural disasters respectively. Swaziland continues to wrestle with a political and economic paradigm that seems to slow its development and the proper distribution of resources. Collectively, as a sub-region, we continue to struggle with the demons of poverty, crime, unemployment, unequal distribution of wealth, shortage of skills and the HIV/AIDS pandemic that is destroying the fabric of our society. Apart from all these major changes in our context, we are also experiencing radical cultural shifts. The cultural makeup of a generation born in South Africa after 1976 is different from that of those born earlier, and the same applies to those born post 1994.

Beneath the visible contesting issues, there is a deeper search for meaning and spirituality around us. Wright (2006: 1–50) explores this search in four areas which he calls 'echoes of a voice': the longing for justice ('a world-put-to-rights'), the quest for spirituality beyond the Church, the hunger for deeper and more meaningful relationships, and an appreciation and delight in the beauty of God's creation. Nolan (2007: 1–2) concurs and goes further to say that not only is there a search but also a level of discomfort with what 'authorities of any kind are saying and have been saying for centuries.' As our context changes, as followers of Christ and as a Church,

> ... we must imagine and pursue the development of new ways of being followers of Jesus ... new ways of doing theology and living biblically, new understandings of mission, new ways of expressing compassion and seeking justice, new kinds of faith communities, new approaches to worship and service, new integrations and conversations and convergences and dreams. (www.emergentvillage.com)

Brian McLaren (2000: 11) captures our agenda as a Church in a postmodern context succinctly: 'If you have a new world, you need a new Church. You have a new world.' As Wesleyans, together with the broader Christian community in Southern Africa, we should embrace the emerging community and culture because they may significantly strengthen our vision of discipleship, the Church and its mission.

This chapter discusses the need for fresh and creative ways that can appropriate the Christian tradition for a postmodern culture. To quote two book subtitles, our challenge as a Church is to seek to proclaim *'Vintage Christianity for New Generations'* (Kimball 2003) and have a *'First Century Passion for the 21st Century World'* (Sweet 2000). Towards this end, we will focus on the need for metaphors and models that can become a liturgy of *healing* and *transformation* in the following issues:

- The need for metaphors of healing and transformation

- How we can 'reframe' our interpretation of scripture for our generation

- How we shape our worship to bring about healing and transformation in our present context

- Some implications for the Methodist Church of Southern Africa.

The need for metaphors of healing and transformation

In the introduction I alluded to two concepts, 'change' and 'postmodernism', and both of these terms have been received with suspicion in many parts of the world. In this section, I try to create a relationship between these concepts and track the transitions that have brought about the world as we know it today. John Dunne once said:

> The holy man of our time, it seems ...[is] a man who passes over by sympathetic understanding from his own religion to other religions and comes again with new insight to his own. Passing over and coming back, it seems, is the spiritual adventure of our time. (1978: ix)

Although Dunne speaks from a comparative religion perspective, I am seeking to embrace postmodern and African concepts of understanding our lived reality in order to make available life-giving resources for the life of our Church. As Dunne (1978) highlights, in order to be prophetic in our time, as in any other time, the ability to move from one's tradition or theological outlook and relate to other theological stances with deep openness unveils a hopeful future for the Church. Put simply, in every culture there is always the tension between the old, the new and the other. The old is the way of shaping reality or cultural practices that seem outdated to at least the younger participants of that culture, quite often mistaken with linear and structured ways of thinking and ordering life. The new is the emergent culture that seems to threaten the former and is usually seen as chaotic and incoherent. The other represents all other forms of religious expression.

TRENDS

Postmodernism has not just mushroomed out of nothing, but is a thought process that has generated itself out of a real context. According to Wright (2002) the world, (the Church included) has gone through various paradigm shifts which began with the Reformation. 'The Reformers protested ... against the way the medieval Church had turned liturgy ... into a quasi-pagan system of magic ritual, which enhanced the power of those who operated it and did little or nothing to let the true gospel shine out' (www.ntwrightpage.com). Since the Reformation, the world has seen the emergence of at least three cultural movements.

First to emerge was the Enlightenment or the 'modern world' as it is often termed. Definitive of this culture is that 'reality was ... conveniently divided up into facts and values; facts were objective and values were subjective ... the individual *could simply* say "I am the master of my fate, I am the captain of my Soul"' (Wright 1999: www.ntwrightpage.com). This era saw the shifting of religious and ethical matters to a private realm and, as such, belief did not matter in the public sphere. The world has paid and is still paying for this strange dichotomy between matters of spirituality and public life. The privatisation of faith has not only historically crippled the Church but continues with its silent undertones as you hear people say 'I do not have anything to do with politics or poverty in the world' – and yet they still regard themselves as active Christians.

Secondly, Wright (2002) claims that the Enlightenment era was followed by what he calls the Romantic movement (the Evangelical movement): 'What matters now is feeling rather than form, the heart rather than the head or body ... it invited you to look within, to see what feelings you had, and to make them the centre of your world, rather than seeing the love of the heart for the true God as the gift of God through the gospel, word, and spirit.' In this one statement, Wright not only defines the culture but also goes further to point out the potential danger therein. When everything about faith looses the integrity of a sound mind rooted in the gospel story, it can easily dwindle into a dark gulf of romanticism.

The last of these cultural shifts is the birth of Existentialism: 'Each of us has inside ourselves a true self which, though long buried, is now to be discovered and enabled to flourish ... what you need if you are an existentialist ... is not to be confronted by the gospel ... but to be helped to discover who you really are' (Wright 2002). Wright further warns that the danger with Existentialism is the rejection of external pressures and the glorification of internal instinct as the true source of authentic existence.

Postmodernism in itself is a product of many shifts in the field of human sciences. There is a mixture of elements which have their roots in one of the above shifts in the processing of knowledge. In my view, Wright's (1999) fundamental argument is that postmodernism seems to deconstruct all the great stories of faith into small individualistic stories that are primarily based on feeling rather than any specific point of view. Something of what he has said is true. Nolan (2006: 182) calls this search for freedom from meta-narratives, the freedom of one's ego. He states 'The attempt at breaking the chains of the past is laudable, but this attempt fails as its only result is to bind us with new chains of egotistical self-centredness' (Nolan 2006: 182). Wright concurs and adds, when '... our controlling narratives, are broken down into little stories: my story, your story, which may be authentic in themselves ... *this* culture is symbolised by the portable personal stereo, creating for its wearer a private and constantly shifting world of sound' (1999).

If we view postmodernism in the latter terms, certainly our generation is bound for destruction by the sound of its own music. At certain levels, there are elements of every culture that need pruning and grafting and this definitely applies with postmodernism. From a positive point of view 'Postmodernism is, in a sense, the rediscovery of the value of human participation, a quest for wholeness and meaning, a perspective on the continuity between all levels of a multi-layered reality' (Herholdt 1998a: 218). This perspective moves us beyond seeing postmodernism as a dark cage of ego worship into the freedom of participating in a relationship with God that helps us discover and create truth at the same time. (Meiring 2005: 32). Herholdt (cited by Meiring 2005: 32) sums it up this way: 'the believer is not called to master abstract truth; rather he or she is challenged to make sense of the world by participating in the creation of a new world in terms of which self can be defined. Faith is therefore my own experience and theology the story or account of my life.'

This seems to take us back to Dunne's theory of passing over to other realities and coming back to define your reality in terms of the multiple lenses through which you have viewed reality. The authentic Christian of our generation will have to make this choice. In all our spheres of thinking about God, living in the world and worshipping God, the challenge is to deal generously with the different strands of our emergent culture. In a practical sense, this binds the older generation to the younger, the fundamentalist and the liberal, the west and the east, Africa and the rest, the traditional with the contemporary, and the literal reader of scripture with the metaphorical reader.

Metaphors of healing

Much of what Jesus is about in the New Testament is redefining God's kingdom through using old and new metaphors. In some places, he invokes the Jewish stories and prophets and in other places he uses the imagery of the ground he stands on at that moment. Scripture employs the images of the Exodus, exile, temple, and empire to shape and reshape the kingdom of God incarnate. Sometimes old metaphors, defined differently in new contexts, give radical contrasts or reversals to the status quo. Jesus, as in the Matthew 13 kingdom parables, piles images on each other to grow the idea of the kingdom in his followers. Nolan (2006: 49–62) suggests that Jesus turned the world of his time upside down. 'His life, his message, and his spirituality were revolutionary. He did not propose a number of improvements to the religious beliefs and practices of his time – like patching up an old garment ... he took the values of his time and turned them on their heads ... he was busy with a social revolution ... that called for a deep revolution' (Nolan 2006: 49–50).

In all that we do as a Church there is a level at which we are a community that turns upside down the images of power, tells stories that create holy reversals, and revitalises the laws of our land with a fervour born of the justice and peace of God.

The truth about Christian belief is that ideas about God and the experience of reality come to life through metaphors. All the 'God talk' of the ages has not come to earth by fax from some other world, but has come through the generations of believers who have faithfully tried to capture in our limited human language a mystery beyond our imagination. For the Church to bring about justice and holiness in our land, it has to use metaphors that form bridges between generations, theologies, different forms of worship, ways of reading scripture, cultures and ultimately our experience of God by faith. Cupitt (1998: 221) contends: 'our world itself is ... a dance of metaphors, pouring out and passing away. We aim only at supplying unifying metaphors that can help people see what we are, what our life is, how we should live, and how we would be completely happy with things as they are.'

Implicit in this discussion is the invitation to review our models of being the Church in order to become relevant to our context. This process of becoming relevant requires a constant journey of unlearning and re-learning new ways of incarnating the gospel in our context. At the very least, this journey towards new metaphors of healing and transformation will involve two aspects of our life as the Church: it calls for new ways of reading the scriptures and new ways of ordering worship.

REFRAMING OUR INTERPRETATION OF SCRIPTURE

The relationship between scripture, the Church and the world in Southern Africa still needs a considerable amount of healing. In an article, Gerald West argues 'The story of the Bible in South Africa, as in most of Africa, is complex and ambiguous: for most people ... many of whom are Christian, the Bible has been both oppressor and liberator; it has supported apartheid and struggled against apartheid; it stands against them and it stands with them'. (West: www.sorat.ukzn.ac.za) In our society today, the Bible is viewed with suspicion from both ends of the interpretative scale. What seems to make it worse is the emergence of the postmodern concepts of viewing the world. A postmodern theologian will not, for instance, approach this already suspicious Bible as if it contains some body of truth ready to be discovered. Postmodern theorist Herholdt (1998b: 476) emphasises that 'truth is therefore not prefabricated, but dynamic and co-determined by the needs, presuppositions, religious background and cultural heritage that the person brings to the Bible'.

With our history as a Church in Southern Africa, we are constantly reminded that our models of interpreting the Bible have life or death consequences; they have the potential to shape the political and social realities of our society (West: www.sorat.ukzn.ac.za). Maybe this is the reason we are quite often reluctant to learn new ways of viewing scripture or even allow our interpretation tools to be challenged. On the other hand, African scholars have made their own strides as they have carried the Bible over the last century and have developed their own methods and tools for reading the Bible (West 1995: 314).

In order to become relevant in our context, it is vital that we retrace the impact that the Bible has had on our African soil and then move on to see what are the challenges that postmodern scholars and theories have posed on these interpretations.

Retracing the journey of interpretation

Justin Ukpong (1999: 314) retraces Africa's journey with the Bible in the modern Church and divides it into three phases:

Phase 1: 1930s–70s: Reactive and apologetic about the place of African culture and hermeneutics; focused on legitimising African religion and culture; dominated by the comparative method.

Phase 2: 1970s–90s: Reactive–proactive method of doing Bible study and theology; use of the African context as resource for biblical interpretation; dominated by Africa-in-the-Bible approach; enculturation–evaluative method and liberation hermeneutics (Black theology).

Phase 3: 1990s onwards: Proactive about doing hermeneutics within the African context; recognition of the ordinary reader; African context as subject of biblical interpretation; dominated by holistic enculturation methodologies.

The 1990s, through the works of universities like the University of KwaZulu-Natal (UKZN) saw the emergence of enculturation hermeneutics, which promoted the reading of Scripture with ordinary readers of the Bible. This model has its own weaknesses but at least it cultivated a culture of reading *with* and not *for* the marginalised of society (West: www.sorat.ukzn.ac.za). Some of this work resonates with the postmodern concept of generating truth in relationship.

This leads us to the ultimate question in this section: How do we interpret Scripture faithfully for our *postmodern* generation?

This question does not have an easy answer but it may be helpful to begin with the basics. It is still important to understand that the Bible is not 'simply a repository of true information about God, Jesus and the hope of the World. It is, rather, part of *the means by which,* in the power of the Spirit, the living God rescues his people and *her* world ...' (Wright 2006: 191). As a valuable book, God intends that we have the Bible, read it, study it, individually and corporately, and bear witness to all of creation about the transforming power of God.

The importance of the Bible in an individual's private life cannot be overemphasized, but the need to develop new ways of reading and interpreting Scripture in public has become an enormous challenge for preachers and worship leaders. James Massey, my Old Testament lecturer at John Wesley College, always said it is time preachers stop hiding the Bible behind the pulpit, pointing fingers at the congregation, and shouting 'Thus says the Lord!' This resonates with the Outcomes-Based Education model because it demystifies the traditional models of scientific learning and makes learning a participatory exercise. As the Church grows in this model of education, the challenge remains: How do we make this relational and participatory model of learning become part of how we do Church? This calls for a scrutiny of the traditional models of interpreting Scripture, preaching and ordering worship. There are a number of issues involved in this challenge: postmodernist views of scripture as a metanarrative, interpreting the text in context, preaching to or preaching with people, and the relationship between scholars and society.

The Metanarrative in context

Historically, scholars have tended to approach their reading of Scripture thematically and use those themes as the organising principles to shape their theology. John Barton (1998: 99–105) cites the following examples: In Eichrodt's work the central principle is the Covenant between God and Israel; for Von Rad it is salvation history as God directs God's people through history; and Brevard Childs' Scripture is tied together by its canonical shape. Amongst our modern scholars, N.T. Wright argues that the whole of Scripture is centred around the motif of creation. So creation moves from the garden in the book of Genesis to the garden in the book of Revelation (Wright 2006: 217–237). In response to this method of interpreting Scripture, postmodernists question the totalising nature of metanarratives and argue that, for

> ... metanarratives ... to accommodate widely diverging local histories and traditions, [they] abstract the meaning of those traditions, by way of a 'translation' into the terms of the master code, which leaves the specific tradition simply unrecognisable. Such metanarratives also become coercive and normative: they systematically distort the local under the sign of the universal. Such a drive to totality cannot respect the specificities of the genuinely heterogeneous traditions. (White 2000: 48–49)

I think White makes at least two good points. He asserts the individuality of people and context. Each context needs to establish its own relationship with any narrative in a way that embraces its individuality and still maintain a relationship of integrity with the wider story or world. I reckon African scholars will agree with the fact that for a long time Africans have interpreted their stories through the lenses of either colonialists or scholars from the west. Postmodernism frees biblical scholars from the quest for the 'right reading' and directs them to a more relational and participatory study of the Bible (West 2008). This does not seem new to the African world view in which there are not many dichotomies in the processing of knowledge and faith. Viewing Scripture as a metanarrative is helpful because it gives us a universal picture of God's dream, but we are to deconstruct and interpret it within a real context in which text, tradition and the participants themselves are in constant dialogue.

STRUCTURING AND RESTRUCTURING WORSHIP

As a Church, our relationship with God, other communities and faith groups, and with the world, is to a great extent an extension of our concepts of God and understanding of worship. Basic to the definition of worship is the idea of acknowledgement and celebration of the value of the one we worship (Wright 2006: 144). As human beings, we are called to put together words and symbols that express the otherness of God in the world. Through our actions of private and public worship, we are in a way generating actions, words, rituals and liturgies that express the alternative world of grace. Wright (2006: 142–146) paints a dramatic picture as found in the book of Revelation chapters 4 and 5, and argues that worship is like eavesdropping on the sweet sounds of heaven and praying that what we hear should become true for this world. According to Wright (2006: 219) true worship should do at least three things:

- As stated above, worship should mould the participant to the image of the one worshipped.

- The worship of God should set one towards the journey of becoming 'more truly human'.

- Through worship and the living out of faith, heaven and earth should overlap.

To pick up the last point, at least from Wright's theological framework of creation, the Church becomes the overlap between heaven and earth because,

within its life, the past meets the present and calls all towards a new earth
and new heaven (Revelation 21). This makes it very important for the Church
to constantly analyse how we worship, particularly because, when we do it, it
is as if we are simply throwing into the air our images of life and of God.

In this section, I will concentrate on a few aspects of public worship,
which will take us directly into what happens in our Church buildings on
Sunday and at other times in the week. Doing so does not mean that the
definition of worship is limited to what happens in sanctuaries, because
worship is a way of life that cannot be bound to a structure.

The Methodist Church, along with other churches in Southern Africa, continues to wrestle with its models of worship. In some parts of the
Church, you find yourself immersed in a liturgy that is largely a translation
of our Anglican heritage. Sometimes if the leader changes one aspect of that
liturgy the congregation will immediately express dissatisfaction. In other
parts of the Church, you might find yourself in what seems like some form
of rock concert, which does not seem to have any formal or written liturgies – sometimes called contemporary worship. In many parts of the world,
this has grown through the ministry of communities like Hillsong. If you
enter some urban churches and wait around for a few hours on a Sunday
you could easily believe you are in two different parts of the world. In the
morning, you will find yourself in the midst of a white congregation, perhaps with a choir and a conductor, or with a worship team with drums and
guitars. A few hours later on the same premises, you will be in the midst of
a black congregation singing hymns with accompaniments such as drums,
whistles and a small pillow. In a few places, you may find mixed congregations where even the languages used in worship are mixed. Quite recently
while on holiday in Swaziland I met a family who cross the border and drive
about 50 kilometres to get to church every Sunday because no one caters for
them in the local churches. These are just a few examples of the expression
of public worship in our culture. The Church surely needs to constantly
look at itself honestly in this regard in order to build a level of integrity.

Leonard Sweet (2005) introduced a seminar with the following remark:
'In order for things to stay the same they must change'. Sweet summed up
his seminar with three basic challenges for the Church. The Church needs
a 'new frame' – a new way of doing worship that is not based on principle

but on images and metaphors that are generated from the tension between social, cultural and religious change, as well as the changes in human beings. The second challenge for the Church is to find a 'big dream' that is relevant for a world that is image and metaphor based. On this basis, Sweet argues that Jesus reframed the religion of his time by transforming the images of his day into Kingdom metaphors and challenged his people to shift from a paradigm that is principle based into prophetic imagination. Finally, he argues that our churches are not filled with people who want to be an audience, but people who want to be participants – people with 'an emotional commitment'. Then the question is: How can we constantly increase the quality of participation in our congregations?

Worshipping in an EPIC way

In his book, *Post Modern Pilgrims,* Leonard Sweet (2000) introduces what he calls the EPIC Church. He argues that for the Church to be relevant in our postmodern times it needs to be Experiential, Participatory, Image-driven and Connected.

Experiential

Sweet believes that for the Church to change it needs to become more experiential and less propositional in its liturgy. He uses a metaphor of two signs with arrows: 'The right arrow says, "this way to heaven"; the left arrow says, "this way to a discussion about heaven." The modernist took the fork to the discussion.' (Sweet 2000: 31) On the same line of thought, Sweet (2000: 31) continues to say that as the modernists discuss heaven, the postmodernists are experiencing heaven. Inasmuch as he seems to highlight the importance of an emotional engagement with the gospel for the future of the Church, it is important that our faith experiences are not a mere romanticism. Particularly within our Wesleyan tradition, experience is not the final arbiter of truth. For experience to truly find its life it needs to be moderated by scripture, tradition and reason.

Participatory

Gone are the days when preachers would say 'We preach it/You hear it':

'Every congregation must become a participant–observer congregation'. (Sweet 2000: 72). In the African philosophy of life, the concept of participation is not new, particularly with most of the African Independent Churches, who shape most of their lives around rituals (Thorpe 1991: 110). Through these different rituals, communities are able to foster community, challenge evil and rebel against forces that destroy community. The strength in this pattern of life is that in the shaping of faith and life all people become participants (Meiring 2005: 181–182).

This culture seems to be part of the younger generation in the Church. At a youth service I attended I felt a bit out of place because the service had so many leaders and participants which made it seem chaotic, and yet everything seemed to fit together neatly at the end. This revealed a different side to what worship can be about. As the Church, we have always used a simple model of worship: we sing and pray together, the Word is read and preached *to us* and we celebrate the sacraments. Sweet (2005) seems to suggest that in our image-driven world 'doing Church' needs to become a different experience from the traditional 'one-person' show where the leader does everything. Can I take this a little further and challenge preachers to open the door for congregants to participate even in their preparation? Preparation for worship will then not be limited to what happens privately in the study. Instead preachers may have to learn to exegete and preach *with* their congregation.

Exegeting metaphors may make this easier. The sermon is no longer just a product of the preacher but a conversation of the preacher, the congregation and the spirit of God. According to Cosby and McClurg (2008):

> To be the Church means we are living the unfolding story of God in the world. We open ourselves to God's continuing newness, to unexpected twists and turns of the plot, to all the drama and comedy and suspense that God wants to write. Our small story is part of a much larger story, the ongoing story of God's little struggling band of followers, and we are either a part of that narrative or a part of the world's narrative.

Image-driven

Sweet takes a rather extreme view of this by implying that words are becoming irrelevant in our image-driven world of mass media. All language is image-based, and words are merely signifiers of the reality being communicated. Scripture is full of symbolism and imagery. The Church does use, and has always used, images to teach the Word and Sacraments as symbols of a greater reality. The Bread and the Wine represent the Body and Blood of Christ. Baptism illustrates the death, burial and resurrection of Christ, and how we have died to our old self and been raised a new person. Images are an important aspect of our worship and will always be. What remains the challenge for the Church is how we continually adapt this old truth in our new world. In 1959 P Smits wrote: 'if Christian faith would that somebody else must die for my sins, and that God requires that for my salvation, I refuse to accept that. It is against all human dignity and responsibility. If that be Christian faith, please, give my portion to the dog' (in Van de Beck 2004: 37). The blood image in Scripture for instance, has many connotations and for many South Africans it raises issues of their political history. Whatever reason Smits came to such a conclusion, it is important for the Church to always assess the relevance and the implications of the images we use because they not only project our theology but also speak differently for each generation.

The gift that comes with the use of imagery is that it begins to connect the real word with the proclamation of Scripture and allows us to go into history and see how those images have been used in the history of the Church. A classical example is the *Rite of Reconciliation* liturgy (SACC March 1996) used by Churches during and after the Truth and Reconciliation Commission (TRC). This rite invokes images used in Scripture such as water, fire, blood, goats, oil, spears, knobs and blankets. These symbols and the images crafted around them are both traditional and also very contextual in terms of South African history. In this regard Smit (in Meiring 2005: 732) urges that liturgy holds the key to the development of theology and that new theological insight relies on creative liturgies that are deeply entrenched in the social and linguistic context of the participants. For instance, when designing a liturgy for a rural farming community you cannot loosely use images from urban contexts.

If images have such a potential to shape our vision of ourselves, our cir-cumstances, as well as our images of God, it is important that as communi-ties we do not abdicate the responsibility of shaping worship to the clergy alone, or to the Church choir or worship leaders and teams. I suggest we let the planning and the shaping of services of worship become a collective responsibility, such that the actual act of worship becomes a combination of images discerned by the body of worshipping people. Some congrega-tions around the world and locally have already seen this as a major element of proclamation and contextualisation of the gospel. For many mainline Churches in Southern Africa, as in other parts of the world, this work has become critical because there is a need to generate models of worship that integrate congregations in terms age, race, economic demographics, gender, class and culture. The role of the Church then is to be the place where alter-native images of being are generated and upheld. This will create an alterna-tive community of integration that is deeply Christ-centred. In the gospels Jesus always seems to generate images that bring the rich and the peasant to the same dinner table, Jews and gentiles in obedience to the same God, and various other opposites together: the fundamentalists and the liberals, the pious and the sinful, the healthy and the sick. In Jesus is revealed the truth that the whole world belongs to God with no disparities.

Connected
In his final point, Sweet (2000: 112) argues that 'Postmoderns want partici-pation at a deeply personal level but at the same time [want a] communal experience of the divine and the transformation of life that issues from that identification with God.' This highlights the need for a relational under-standing of the Church – the personal relationship with God, neighbour and the world. This is not only Scriptural but also part of our Wesleyan heritage. The belief is in the 'growing of saints' through relationships of accountability. Griffith (1995: 137) explores the need for people to tell their personal stories of who God may or may not be for them. He suggests there is always room for new stories about God: 'it is in the context of intimate interactions that a person continues to co-create an evolving story with God that is uniquely his or her own ... not dominated by *other* stories ... religious doctrines ... nor psychological *theories*' (Griffith 1995: 137). Al-though Griffith speaks from a narrative therapy perspective, it is vital that

in our communities we cultivate the culture of telling personal narratives of our experience of God. In some cases, the telling of people's stories may not be limited to small groups but may take place in Church services specifically designed as spaces for telling stories. In cases where such sacred spaces have been opened, people have had the opportunity to not only tell their stories, but be transformed by them.

One of the gifts that came out of the South African TRC was that it not only functioned as a reconciliation liturgy but also promoted a culture of confession. Inasmuch as there are so many debates around the success of the TRC, there are visible traces of the fact that post-apartheid South Africa is a confessing society (Posel 2006: 8). Eriksson (2000: 34) takes this thought further to give a liturgical interpretation of the process of telling stories. Through storytelling, lamenting and cleansing rituals, the perpetrators could confess, repent, and receive and give forgiveness. On the other hand, the victims could hear the truth, envision justice and work towards restoration of relationships. Over and above the merits and demerits of the process, the TRC reveals a participatory way of dealing with the pain and hurts of people. I believe that the Church is well placed in society to create spaces for confession and affirmation and growth. The question is how well we as a Church provide sacred spaces where people can reframe their story of faith, get in touch with God's big dream, and become participants rather than spectators.

Looking at the politics of the post-apartheid South Africa, there is a sense in which historic images and metaphors of communication still dominate and regulate how people speak about their past and, consequently, their future: 'truth telling ... rooted in the TRC, holds that political and personal liberation – being free – is quintessentially about the space for confession: to transcend the past and enter into a space of common humanity, defined by our propensity to pain and compassion' (Posel 2006: 9). The Church has to constantly work towards 'taking apart' (Morgan 2000: 45) the beliefs, ideas and practices of our contemporary society in order to open space for 'alternative stories that assist people to challenge and break' (Morgan 2000: 49) paradigms that hinder and stagnate healing and transformation in society. It takes the faithfulness of the Church to contribute towards dealing with the culture of violence, the levels of poverty and the challenges of crime in our society.

IMPLICATIONS FOR SOUTHERN AFRICAN METHODISM

Having discussed some of the emerging issues in the interpretation of Scripture and the ordering of our worship, we must consider some of the implications for our Church. These thoughts are not necessarily new as some Methodist scholars in the Southern African region have already pointed out. The most recent is Peter Storey's (2004) book, *And are we yet Alive: Revisioning our Wesleyan heritage in the New Southern Africa*. What comes through in most of our recent documents dating back to the *Obedience 81* conference, or indeed even further back, is the need to rediscover models of ministry that encourage every member's participation in the shaping of our structures and also facilitate practical ways of being disciples. Storey (2004: 17) calls this working towards 'an outcomes based theology'. One of the implicit issues in this paper is a search for models of reading 'Scripture and great texts from the Christian tradition with attentiveness, nuanced with understanding, humility and a lively imagination' (Duke University Divinity School Curriculum, cited Storey 2000: 59). Inasmuch as postmodernism offers very liberating principles in the way we interact with Scripture, we should be careful that we do not land ourselves in a form of romanticism and ego-worship.

Listening to some of the voices in the discussion around same-sex relationships, it sounds as if part of the debate is a clash of hermeneutical methods and paradigms. Some scholars have opted to work from a fixed metanarrative, quite often from a deontological viewpoint, and others from a postmodern view that deconstructs all reality and romanticises experience. Postmodernism needs to spread its wings beyond experience and reason into engagement with Scripture as a metanarrative. The engagement between the modern and traditional models of interpretation of Scripture will give birth to the 'narrative of *transformation*' (Storey 2004: 19). Perhaps, wisdom is to be found in learning to move beyond one's paradigm of interpretation into another, and then to return with new lessons, allowing this openness to be part of our celebration of diversity.

The second challenge in this article is the need for metaphors that can become vehicles of our mission imperatives. This takes the Church into the heart of the world. As we look at the images of power, sex, money and mass media, we are called to turn these weapons of destruction into 'plough-shares' for the sake of the Kingdom of God. I do not believe that this will be possible if the liturgies that we use in our communities are over 50 years old. There is enormous value in these liturgies but some of them are still foreign in the images they use. A good example is the Book of Common Prayer used in many of our African congregations. The work of healing and transformation requires the crafting of new liturgies, hymns and orders of service that embrace our rich cultural diversity. Can the loss of young people in our Churches be attributed to this shortcoming?

The third essential for the Church of the future is the ability to communicate the good news to a generation that no longer wants to be a mere audience. Teaching and preaching in this context, where information about Scripture and the Church is available to all, ordained and lay, has become a critical task. Can the sermon and church service become a place of interaction and participation? Can it become a meeting of the skills of good communication and creative listening? Can it become a participatory drama immersed in people's stories of celebration and pain? If this is a possibility, we need to constantly analyse and vary our pulpit ministry with new and radical alternatives. Our new outcomes model of teaching is a great tool in equipping our ministers for this task.

Wright (2006) has written quite extensively about the loss and disregard of beauty. He argues that the Church needs to rediscover the beauty of not only the aesthetics of our church buildings, but also the beauty that comes to us through the arts. If the Church is to grow towards a more experiential and participatory form of worship, we need to rediscover the beauty of the variety of musical expressions, from both early Church and the postmodern world. The world around us awakens our senses and imaginations with its wide variety of youthful expressions of colour, dance, poetry and language. As we rediscover this beauty of creation, we will be getting in tune with a context that seems to have evolved faster than the Church.

Peter Storey plainly states that 'people who do not *worship* together, *can never be one*.' The concept of oneness is very challenging for a Church that exists in a racialised society. Villafañe (1995: 57–58) argues that the challenge for the Church is to work towards a biblical posture of a 'racial shalom' (peace – with its rich biblical meaning of healing, harmony, reconciliation, welfare, wholeness, and justice). It is a prophetic challenge to the Church to be the 'space' where the presence and contribution of believers of all colours could be seen as 'light' and could be savoured as 'salt' in a broken world ... to be a sign of the kingdom of God – a place where transformed relations and the presence of justice could be modelled.

And this is all the more so because many congregations are happy to be 'tourists' rather than 'pilgrims' (Hudson 2005: 32–40) in each other's culture. Tourists view a culture from the outside; pilgrims journey with those cultures. My colleague Alan Storey often uses the term 'hospitality' to express the attitude that we should have towards each other. White congregations and black congregations must learn what it means to be hospitable to other cultures in their worship. This form of hospitality is not a simple one but sometimes involves a profoundly painful and compassionate journey. It means the Church should work towards common images, symbols and metaphors, both old and new, to bring about healing and transformation. These images have to call us towards a greater awareness of the reality of God's Kingdom dawning 'on earth as it is in heaven'.

CONCLUDING REMARKS

In this article, I have endeavoured to discuss the subject of postmodernism in our African context and sought to discover lessons and relationships with our Church in Southern Africa. It seems to me that our mission objective as the MCSA, as recently captured by the Umtata Mission Congress Report (January 2005) can be realised through a variety of strategies. My hope is that this paper will stimulate conversation and lead to courageous action as we respond to these challenges together. Listening to the voices coming out of the Mission Congress there is a reiteration of the need to find new models of being the Church in Southern Africa. In the first section of this article I have encouraged the reading of Scripture *with* instead of *for* the people, because this will encourage an *incarnational* way of engaging with Scripture. The Scriptures will no longer belong to the academic readers but become a shared entity.

In the second section, I have ventured into the field of liturgy and briefly looked at the framework of our worship. New liturgies and ways of leading worship will surely break down all the dualisms: sacred/secular, public/private, mind/body, faith/reason, that emerged with the Enlightenment. As Gibbs and Bolger (2005: 67) put it, 'For emerging churches, there are no longer any bad places, bad people, or bad times. All can be made holy. All can be given to God in worship. All modern dualisms can be overcome.' Postmodernism cuts across this compartmentalisation that enables people to be 'spiritual while leaving their secular lives untouched.' (Gibbs & Bolger 2005: 77) For emerging spirituality, no aspect of our lives should remain untouched by God.

If these models are explored faithfully we will surely be working towards alternative communities. Such communities will seek to constantly live out a Christ-centred life that challenges all forms of discrimination. This community will be modelled by: the rich sharing the same dining table as the poor; the sick and vulnerable (such as people living with HIV/AIDS) being listened to and not judged; different races celebrating their differences together. As John and Charles Wesley used powerful biblical stories and imagery in their hymns and liturgies, this alternative community will experiment with diverse worship styles, new liturgies and narratives seeking to be faithful to biblical narrative, tradition and reason, yet still honouring their experience of Jesus. This 'is not to claim to have the truth captured, stuffed, and mounted on the wall. It is rather to be in a loving ... community of people who are seeking the truth ... on the road of mission ... and who have been launched on the quest by Jesus, who, with us, guides us still' (McLaren 2004: 293).

BIBLIOGRAPHY

Barton, J 1998. Old Testament Theology in Rogerson, J (ed). *Beginning Old Testament Study*. St. Louis: Chalice

Cosby, N G & McClurg, K *Becoming the Authentic Church, wp.theoblogical.org, 2008-02-08*

Cupitt, D 1998. Post-Christianity, in Heelas Paul (ed) *Religion, Modernity and Postmodernity,* 218–232, Oxford: Blackwell Publishers

Dunne, J S 1978. *The way of all the earth: Experiments in Truth and Religion.* Notre Dame: University of Notre Dame Press

Eriksson, B 2000. *The Truth and Reconciliation Commission: A Liturgy of Reconciliation in South Africa.* Orebro Theological Seminary (Unpublished). www.missioncouncil.se – 2007 -12- 18

Gibbs, E & Bolger, R K 2005. *Emerging Churches: Creating Christian Community in Postmodern Cultures.* Grand Rapids: Baker

Griffith, M E 1995. 'Opening therapy to conversations with a personal God'. In Weingarten, K (ed). *Cultural resistance: Challenging beliefs about men, women and therapy.* New York: Harrington Park Press

Herholdt, M D 1998a. Post modern Theology, in Maimela, Simon & Konig, Adrio (eds), *Initiation into Theology: The Rich Variety of Theology and Hermeneutics,* 215-229. Pretoria: J L van Schaik

Herholdt, M D 1998b. Post modern Hermeneutics, in Maimela, Simon & Konig, Adrio (eds), *Initiation into Theology: The Rich Variety of Theology and Hermeneutics,* 451-470. Pretoria: J L van Schaik

Hudson, T 2005. *A Mile in My Shoes: Cultivating Compassion.* Nashville: Upper Room Books

Kimball, D 2003. *The Emerging Churches: Vintage Christianity for New Generations.* Grand Rapids: Zondervan.

McLaren, B D 2000. *The Church on the Other Side: Doing Ministry in the Post modern Matrix.* Grand Rapids: Zondervan.

McLaren, B D 2004: *A Generous Orthodoxy.* Grand Rapids: Zondervan

Meiring, A M 2005. From Christianity to African Religion and back again. *Verbum et Ecclessia* 26 (3): 718–739

Meiring, A M 2005. Heart of Darkness: A deconstruction of traditional Christian concepts of reconciliation by means of religious studies perspective on the Christian and African Religions, unpublished DD thesis, University of Pretoria

Morgan, A 2000. *What is narrative therapy?* Easy-to-read introduction. Adelaide: Dulwich Centre Publications.

Nolan, A 2006. *Jesus Today: A Spirituality of Radical Freedom*. Cape Town: Double Storey Books

Posel, D 2006. The Post Apartheid Confessional, Reasons of Faith, religion in modern public life, *The Wiser Review*, Number two, December 2006, p.8–9

Storey, P 2004. *And are we yet Alive: Revisioning our Wesleyan Heritage in the New Southern Africa*. Cape Town: Methodist Publishing House

Sweet, L 2000. *Post-Modern Pilgrims: First Century Passion for the 21st Century World*. Nashville: Broadman & Holman

Thorpe, S A 1991. *African Traditional religions*. Pretoria: Unisa

Villafañe, E 1995. *Seek the Peace of the City: Reflections on urban Ministry*. Grand Rapids: William B. Eerdmans

West, G O 1995. *Biblical Hermeneutics of liberation. Modes of reading the Bible in South African context*. 2nd ed. Pietermaritzburg: Cluster Publications Ukpong, JS 1999. Developments in Biblical Interpretation in Modern Africa, *Missolonia* 27 (3), 313–329

West, G O (SA) *Reading the Bible in Africa: Constructing our own Discourse*. www.sorat.ukzn.ac.za, 2008-01-08

White, D G 2000. The Scholar as mythographer: Comparative Indo-European Myth and Postmodern Concerns, in Patton, KC & Ray, BC (eds), *A Magic Still Dwells, Comparative Religion in a postmodern Age*, University of California Press

Wright, N T 2002. *Freedom and Framework, Spirit and Truth: Recovering Biblical Worship*, www.ntwrightpage.com, 2008-01-05

Wright, N T 1999. *The Bible for the Post Modern World*, www.ntwrightpage.com, 2008-01-10

Wright, N T 2006. Simply Christian – Why Christianity makes sense. New York: Harper Collins

INSIDERS OR OUTSIDERS?

Pastoral care with Christian gay women in a local Methodist congregation

Debbie van de Laar

INTRODUCTION

1994 was a watershed year in the life of all South Africans. Not only did the new democracy bring political freedom to all people of this land, but the new constitution also brought rights to many who had never before experienced the protection they offer. Not least of these marginalised groups was the gay community. These, our brothers and sisters, began to ask the church for the same acceptance that the state now offered them. Then, on 29 November 2006, the Civil Union Act was passed, which for the first time allowed people of the same gender to enter into legal 'civil partnerships'. No longer could the ministers of churches dodge the question: as marriage officers, the state would allow us to conduct 'civil unions'. The question was, would the church allow us to do so?

Voices both within and outside the variety of religious institutions in South Africa have for many years challenged (and continue to challenge) faith communities to take the need for gay and lesbian Christian relation-ships and spirituality very seriously. Some churches, like the Reforming Church, gladly accepted the state's offer for their ministers to be registered with the Department of Home Affairs in order that they may conduct civil union ceremonies for gay couples. Others, like the Methodist Church of Southern Africa (hereafter referred to as the MCSA), have not accepted this offer from the state. The MCSA has been in dialogue over this issue for many years, but has not yet found agreement.

It began with a call from ministers for guidance on this issue. Aware that the majority of Christians believe homosexuality to be 'a sin', some ministers also realise that many people in same-sex relationships feel that they may need to leave the church in order to become whole. Not wanting these peo-ple to feel like 'outsiders', some of those ministers silently, but routinely, offer services of blessing for people in same-sex relationships. At the same time, other ministers, fearing that a loss of 'standards', or morality in the church would not be helpful to the church's witness, will neither bless these rela-tionships, nor allow the people in them a place in the leadership of church life. In response to this call for guidance from the ministers, Conference (the highest decision making body in the MCSA) mandated the Doctrine, Ethics and Worship Committee of the MCSA (hereafter referred to as DEWCOM) to begin to explore the issue. They put together an initial draft paper which they presented to Conference 2001 (DEWCOM 2001), which began a process of dialogue which continues to the present day. The MCSA does not at present have a policy with regard to gay issues, beyond the virtu-ally unanimous support of the foundational conviction that as a church 'we are to be a community of love rather than rejection' (DEWCOM 2003: 2).

This guiding belief is based on watching the ways in which Jesus, espe-cially in the gospel of Luke, included marginalised people such as lepers, women and children. 'On the ground', however, amongst lay people as well as amongst many of our ministers, there is a widespread belief that homo-sexuality is 'perverted', and that gay people are 'outsiders', in the same camp as paedophiles or prostitutes. The broader leadership of the MCSA appears to fall anywhere in between the poles of total acceptance, and complete re-jection. These varied positions obviously reflect a variety of theologies that have led to these conclusions.

As the MCSA, therefore, our obvious task is to *reflect* on this praxis, in order to do the theology that our congregations are asking of us. Understanding this need for reflection led me into research using a narrative, pastoral approach.

It began as I invited a group of six articulate, assertive, professional women in their thirties and forties (who all attended the church at which I was a minister) to join me as research participants. I knew each woman was both gay and deeply committed to following Christ. Together we engaged in a series of group meetings using narrative conversations to collaboratively produce written research reports.

This feminist, contextual, participative action research is the beginning of what must necessarily be a careful and perhaps even slow process, as we allow our stories to intersect and to have congruency with the stories of the bible. Only then will it be possible for the participants to co-construct alternative, preferred stories of an inclusive Christian spirituality, and ultimately a theology that both integrates the sexual stories of our lives into spiritual stories of our lives, and also integrates 'outsiders' into the church.

During the course of our research together, we women found that four questions formed the central strands of all of our narrative conversation. They were:

1. How have you integrated the spiritual and sexual stories of your life?

2. How has your picture of God changed during this process?

3. How has your experience of the church and its pastoral care impacted this process of integrating the spiritual and sexual stories of your life?

4. What are your feelings about 'standing up'? (We let each research participant define for herself what she would like to 'stand up' to, but, for most of us, this referred to a justification of gay orientation and practice.)

What follows is a shortened record of the narrative conversations the group shared concerning these topics. In each section I begin by outlining some of the unhelpful discourses with which we, as research participants, came to the group meetings. I will then describe the practices that lead us to being able to 're-story' (White & Epston 1990: 14) the impact of these discourses on our lives.

STORIES OF SPIRITUAL AND SEXUAL INTEGRATION

The first question which formed a central strand to many of our conversations during the group meetings was the question: 'How have you integrated the spiritual and the sexual stories of your life?'

Dominant Discourses Surrounding the Integration of the Sexual and Spiritual Stories of Christian Gay Women

All the research participants spoke of the difficulty which they had in integrating the sexual and the spiritual stories of their lives. Maggi, for example, spoke about how difficult this was because she had believed and internalised the church's very powerful discourse of sin and was trapped in guilt. She spoke of how hard it was for her that the church believed that 'being gay is immoral, or wrong or evil', and that it saw heterosexuality as the only option. O'Neill and Ritter (1992: 213,214) explain that this difficulty with being perceived as evil complicates the 'coming out process', as Christian gay people 'become convinced that they are indeed evil and contaminated'. Maggi also spoke of the ways in which her parents' initial shocked disapproval of her being gay made it harder for her to integrate the story of her sexuality and her spirituality. The discourses of sin, contamination and evil created 'a personal discomfort' in her.

It was partly this sense of being judged and oppressed that kept Des on the fringes of the faith community. She particularly rejected the discourse in the church that suggested that only if one is heterosexual, is one free to explore and enjoy one's sexuality 'normally'. She said that if you are gay, that expression of sexuality is considered abnormal, and so teens who consider themselves gay are sent to see psychologists to talk about their sexual expression in the hope of changing it. However, 'straight' teenagers are free to explore their sexuality 'normally'. Des objected to the way in which this practice, instigated by a restrictive discourse, contributes to gay teenagers rejecting a faith community (and thus their spirituality) as a step to protect themselves, rather than having to reject 'themselves' and what they see to be true for themselves.

Des told us how these oppressive discourses and practices spoke so loudly in her life, that when she, at nineteen, acknowledged to herself that she was gay, she determined that she would 'never act on it' in order to protect herself and her family from the pain of rejection that she knew would be inevitable. When she finally did confront the discourse and act in accordance with her sexual orientation, then 'being gay', as she had feared, did do some terrible damage, especially in her relationship with her mother. From then on, for a few years, what Des termed 'healing with Mom' became a top priority for her, and was, happily, eventually accomplished. Des made it clear, however, that none of this pain was helpful to her in integrating her sexuality and spirituality. The discourse and practices stemming from this only brought pain and suffering.

Pixie identified with Des and Maggi's experiences of the discourse of shame that results in church and family rejection of gay people. As a child she watched another child be teased for being a 'lesbo' and learned something about shame. Her parents' disgust in response to Pixie's childhood questions about lesbianism, taught her more about how powerful the discourse of shame surrounding homosexuality is. During the group conversations Pixie described how she had learned to 'compartmentalise' her life, keeping her gay, church and music friendships quite separate, in order to avoid shame and disrespect.

Alternative Stories of Integration of the Sexual and Spiritual Stories of Christian Gay Women

Stories of Love

Maggi, having thought very deeply about both her faith and her sexuality, had done a lot of personal, social and biblical analysis to counteract the dominant discourses of society regarding gay people. The first, and probably most powerful alternative story that she had generated, which had helped her to integrate the story of her sexuality and her spirituality, was the one surrounding her falling in love with Carolyn. She was curious about why, if according to certain interpretations of the Bible, God hated homosexuality, God would bring her back to Godself through a gay relationship. She wondered why it was that when she was in this gay relationship that she experienced God's blessing in her love, both with Carolyn and with their two children, Liam and Andrea. She experienced this 'blessing' as being the same kind of joy and peace that 'only Christ can bring', that she had first experienced when she had been attending an Anglican youth organisation as a teenager. At that stage she was not yet even faintly aware of her sexual orientation.

Bernice was interested in this idea of God calling Maggi into relationship through her gay lover. Bernice noted that it was also, ironically, through her gay relationship with Des that she had first redeveloped her relationship with God. Pixie was also interested by the way in which God called the research participants back through their gay partners, but in a different way. She only became a Christian after she had known for most of her life that she was gay. She said that it was becoming a Christian that had helped her 'to feel at home in her own skin'. She also spoke of 'the joy and good that has come out of my relationship with Theresa', and quoted a Rod Stewart song that described her feelings about being with Theresa: 'If loving you is wrong, then I don't want to be right'. This experience of being 'at home in her own skin' relates almost exactly to Corn's (1995: 216) expression of his experience, when he said, 'I didn't feel comfortable as a gay man until after I became a Christian'. Carolyn told us that the closer she got to Maggi, the closer she got to God.

So it seems that the profound love experiences that all of the research participants of the group had experienced were very helpful in the authentic integration of their sexual and spiritual stories. Empereur (1998: 4) tells us that sexuality and spirituality are no longer at odds with each other when we stop asking 'is it right or wrong?' and begin to ask 'to what extent is my life a loving one?' Perhaps their experience matched that of Dame Julia of Norwich who states 'in our sensuality, God is' (Ellison 1996: 220). In *Graced, Gifted and Gay*, Frost (2001: 36) says that there is 'no better catalyst for authenticity than irrepressible joy'. The fact that all of the research participants could relate to this alternative 'joyful experience of love' story, and add their own experiences to it, meant that the love story developed a lovely, thick description of God's approval of each of their love relationships (Morgan 2000: 15). As a result, it became a powerful alternative story of caring and mutuality.

In our group meetings we discovered another powerful alternative story to the dominant discourses of shame and judgement that surround gay women in the church. This alternative story revolved around our use of the Bible.

Bible Stories

When, at the age of twenty-eight, Maggi had 'discovered' her gay sexual orientation, she went to see a male Christian psychologist. Together with him, she began to question the ways in which she had read the Bible. He helped her to realise that parts of the Bible, especially the Holiness Code, were written from a different context to the one in which she now found herself. The Holiness Code had been written from a context of war, and the psychologist explained to Maggi that, within that context, the nation did not 'need' gay people. It needed heterosexual people who, through their procreation would increase the tribe numerically, and thus give them the advantage over other groups in the area. In addition, Maggi said that she had discovered that, at the time that the Holiness Code was written, the Israelites did not want to be identified with the religions of the surrounding nations, who allowed homosexuality in the form of temple prostitution. These ideas had helped her to change the way that she was reading and interpreting the Bible. Gerkin (1991: 18) calls this pastoral practice 'retrieving and reinterpreting biblical metaphors and images'. He believes that as we reinterpret the meanings we have assigned to biblical passages and images, we are able to 'relate those meanings to the specifics of the contemporary situation in which the pastor is working'. These explanations helped Maggi not to lose what she refers to as an 'on/off love affair with God'. They helped her to challenge the discourse that states that some interpretations of the Bible say that it is 'wrong' to be gay. While Maggi did not share what her sources for these explanations were, similar views are held by Brash (1995: 39–46) where he reminds us that the Holiness Code 'sets out how the behaviour of the Israelites, as God's chosen people, was to be distinct from that of other nations' (1995: 41). He also reminds us that, because the Israelites believed that a woman was only a 'vessel in which the seed [of a man] developed into a new life', 'any action in which the seeds of a possible new life were wasted was declared to be sinful' (1995: 41).

Jakobsen (1997: 71) speaks of a similar experience to Maggi's, of 'the lights going on' as she 'discovered more progressive interpretations' of scripture, and how these changed her views concerning homosexuality.

Theresa was interested in the participants' responses to the 'problem' of scriptural interpretation. She spoke of how she had for many years disagreed with traditional interpretations of scripture regarding animal sacrifice. As someone committed to animal rights, she couldn't integrate the story of the God she loved and worshipped with a God who could demand the abuse of animals as part of that worship. Then, when Theresa read the Wink (1999) article, she said that she wished she had read it 'twenty years ago' because it helped her to stand against the discourse that uses a particular interpretation of the Bible to judge Christians for being gay. Once again, in the group, she found a different reading of Scripture helping to form a strong story of resistance towards oppressive discourses (Wylie 1994).

These alternative stories, repeated and affirmed in the group, as well as our ways of knowing, helped to contradict and so to heal what McCall Tigert (1996: 72–78) calls 'splitting', 'projective identification' and the 'internalisation of shame'. In our group meetings we shared and reflected on each other's alternative stories of the love of our partners, and the ways in which they had helped us to see that God approved our relationships. We shared different ways of reading Scripture, and those practices helped us to see that God may be less judgemental of us than we had at first thought. McCall Tigert (1996: 115) suggests that 'when persons reflect theologically on the realities of their lives as they actually live them ... then psychological integration is possible. In other words, a theology of liberation leads to a psychology of liberation'. Certainly our group reflections on Scripture, and on our lives, brought us more freedom than, as individuals, we had experienced before.

Pictures of God

The next issue which formed a central strand to many of our conversations was the question 'How has your picture of God changed during the course of our group meetings?' I will begin by exploring some of the discourses with which the research participants came into the research. After this, I will look at ways in which the unhelpful aspects of those discourses were 're-authored' (White and Epston 1990: 13).

Dominant Discourses Surrounding the Pictures of God of Christian Gay Women

I will never forget Theresa's words when we first began the group meetings: 'I feel like a disappointment to God, and God is at my centre'. According to Theresa, this internalisation of the dominant discourses of the church has caused her to feel that she cannot take communion. In the Roman Catholic Church, from where Theresa originally comes and which she loves deeply, 'you have to confess your sins before you take communion'. Since Theresa could not 'stop being gay' and believed that 'who I am is wrong', she excluded herself from this most precious sacramental gift of connection with a God who would really rather die than live without her. She said this feeling of 'not being good enough' to take communion, has prevented her from being as involved in church life as she would have liked, and that she experiences this as a kind of 'loss'. Amideo (1999: 1) agrees that our theology can alienate us from our experience of God, and tells us that 'an antiquated and erroneous theology, nurtured by fear, confronts Christian gays and lesbians with unbearable exclusion ... and spiritual torment'.

Other research participants in the group shared similar stories of feeling cut off from God, because of the discourse that 'homosexual' and 'holy' are incompatible terms (Empereur 1998: 2). Bernice had simply drifted away from the church, and so distanced herself from God, because she didn't feel that she 'fitted in'. When Maggi finally admitted to being gay, and was at last experiencing 'being right' in her relationships with other people, she spoke of finding it hard to reconcile 'being an abomination' with the sense she had of God calling her back into relationship. As Empereur suggests

Maggi initially found it hard to find in her same-sex relationships 'a means of grace' that would help her to move 'towards sainthood' (1998: 2). It must be said though, that her picture of God had been seriously damaged by her introduction, for the first time, at university in Stellenbosch, to people who believed that the Bible taught that apartheid was God-sanctioned. Unable to swallow the belief that God had favourite races, Maggi turned her back on God, writing a one page thesis entitled 'Why God does not Exist'.

This rejection of God, or this feeling of being cut off from God, in my experience, speaks of gay people battling to integrate their sexual and spiritual lives. In fact it is typical of most of us trying to integrate even our heterosexuality with our spirituality. Ind (2003: xiii) speaks of our 'collective discomfort around sexuality'. We live in a society that 'overwhelmingly privileges those who get turned on by people of the other sex' (2003: 32). This centralising of some privileged discourses happens in society, despite homosexuality having been removed from the American Psychological Association's list of mental disorders (McClain-Taylor 1996: 81). In addition, because the Catholic Church has taken such a strong stand on the issue of Natural Law, 'any sex which is not open to the transmission of life (the papal way of describing making babies) is therefore not what God wants' (Ind 2003: 12). This restrictive attitude has silently infiltrated church-talk of all denominations about sexuality, and so 'sexual activity outside of marriage comes to be seen as sinful, and homosexual practice as especially dishonourable' (2003: 13).

As a group, the research participants and I felt that we needed to challenge these negative pictures of God if we, as co-researchers, were to be able to enjoy being with God. Without enjoying spirituality, or finding it inspiring, it would be difficult for the research participants to integrate the stories of their being gay into their spirituality.

Alternative Stories of the Pictures of God of Christian Gay Women

It was Theresa who, in the very first week of her being with us, began the construction of her alternative story of God. She picked up on Maggi's experience that, despite discovering her homosexuality, Maggi had felt God calling her back into a relationship. Theresa said that even at the time she felt that the church was pushing her away, 'God kept calling' to her. Empereur (1998: 33,34) describes her own similar experience this way: 'I always find myself coming back to the church – I desert her, but she is the only mother that I have'.

This picture of God patiently, gently, calling and reaching out was further developed by Carolyn. She spoke of her conversion experience being a very emotional one for her, but one that marked the beginning of a very gentle experience of God. She describes God as 'softly placing night lights' in 'corners of the rooms of her life that have become a little dusty'. These 'dusty' places referred to all sorts of ways in which she could become a more whole person, but have nothing to do with her sexual identity. She described how this experience developed into a 'trusting, loving relationship with Jesus'. This relationship has grown so strong, she is certain that he would tell her if he didn't like her sexual identity. She described her relationship with him as having been developed from the scriptural picture from John 15 of us 'being in Jesus, so that he can be in us'. Gerkin (1991: 16) tells us that one of the goals of pastoral ministry is to understand the metaphorical images that shape our understandings of the Christian life. This gentle metaphor of God as a housekeeper, is certainly one that has shaped Carolyn's experience of God's acceptance of her. The de-institutionalised, personalised way in which Carolyn described the 'night light' story of her picture of God resonates with the importance that feminist theologians give to 'women's own oral traditions, myths and legends as inspiration for [their] spirituality and action' (Isherwood and McEwan 1996: 10). Carolyn's story also serves to confirm that it is entirely possible for gay people to come to wholeness, even in the face of prejudice and suffering.

Des described an experience of driving into Bloemfontein right into an exceptionally beautiful sunset, and then, that night, of reading the book *Conversations with God* (Walsch 1997) and it all 'making sense'. While it is very hard to 'dissect' or even sometimes explain a spiritual experience, it seems that the combination of the awe that Des felt in viewing this particularly beautiful experience, led her to become more aware of God in a positive rather than a judgemental sense. In that state of awe, her reading of the book, helping her to put new words to the ways in which she understood

God, was a particularly profound experience. She described how this experience caused her picture of God to become so much more 'mystery and light and spirit'. Des saw this move away from traditional views of God, associated with 'good and bad', or 'right and wrong', to a new, less judgemental view of a more 'beautiful' God, as particularly healing.

Pixie described her preferred relationship with God as introducing a feeling of peace that she did not feel before, and an emptiness that had been there being 'filled'. Maggi told us that she 'enjoys the light of Christ and the love of God' as a blessing. At the end of our times together, I received a letter from Theresa, in which she wrote:

> I have difficulty in reconciling with myself ... because of how I perceived God sees me. This has been very negative and destructive in my life. I have a sense that this project (referring to the research group meetings) has been 'meant' and that I am at the start of a great personal journey. I feel an increasing awareness of God's love for me, and this is almost too awesome to contemplate ...

I am thrilled that during the course of the research project, we were able to intentionally witness each other's alternative story, which described just how holiness and homosexuality are in fact compatible, and which reminded us that 'Gay sexuality is a fact of creation' (Empereur 1998: 3). In hearing each other's stories of feeling close to God, we witnessed that 'whoever we are and whatever we become, we are loved by God' (Ind 2003: 145).

As a minister, while I am glad that the research participants individually experienced God's closeness, I am also concerned about their communal experience of God. Marshall (1994: 74) says that 'individual spiritual and sexual dynamics cannot be separated from the broader community of faith for the lesbian, gay or bisexual person', because as 'one's sexual orientation is oppressed and devalued in the name of God, one's spiritual life is at risk'. And so it is that we needed to move on to consider a more community-oriented experience of sexuality and spirituality.

PASTORAL CARE – MAKING THE CHURCH A SAFER PLACE

The research participants taught me that it is one thing to experience the love of God privately, but it is an altogether different and more difficult thing to worship God amongst a congregation of people whom one may feel are passing judgement – and it was just this that formed the third major strand of conversation in our group meetings. The question I asked each of the research participants was 'How has your experience of the church and its pastoral care impacted the process of your integration of the sexual and spiritual stories of your life?' Once again, I will begin by considering some of the experiences of the research participants prior to the start of the group meetings. From there I will move on to consider ways in which we resisted the discourses of homophobia in the church. Halperin (1995: 30) believes that it is this resistance that alters the dynamics of personal struggle. I believe that the experience of the group validates his assertion, as I will outline below.

Dominant Discourses Surrounding the Pastoral Care of Christian Gay Women

Another of the four areas that we focused on in our research group meetings was the research participant's experience of pastoral care. Reinharz (1992: 234), in her desire to free up creativity in research, allows for an unusual realm of study, the study of 'unplanned human experience'. In this section, I would like to explore the dominant discourses of an unplanned event that happened in the lives of Maggi, Carolyn, Liam and Andrea during the course of our research together. Because there is a Methodist Church much closer to them than the church they usually attended, and because it is a multi-racial, but predominantly black, congregation, Maggi and Carolyn decided to visit there one Sunday. They felt that it would be good for their coloured children to find some role models of 'their' colour, and were considering moving there permanently. Knowing that the community was a multi-racial one led them to expect that it would be open to minority groups. That week the regular minister was not preaching. In his place was a local preacher, who told the congregation that the country was 'going to the dogs' because 'we are not holding onto God's laws. Men are trying to be women and women are trying to be men'. He said this in reference to media reports of a gay couple who had gone to court over a disputed surrogate parenthood case. The preacher's obvious heterosexism made it clear that he had internalised the church's discourse that being homosexual is an abomination. Knowing that the preacher believed them to be 'abominable' was extremely hurtful for Maggi and Carolyn. What was even more hurtful was the fear that this preacher might cause Maggi and Carolyn's children to begin to view their parents as 'abominable'.

This incident highlights how 'unsafe' a place the church can be for gay people. And yet it does not have to be. Corn (1995: 216) came to a place of self-acceptance with regard to being gay, partly through, he says, 'the love and support of a particular congregation'. The church that Maggi and Carolyn attended that day was not 'a welcoming, caring fellowship' in which people grow and where 'homophile people know that you are committed to accepting and supporting them as fully as any other members of the church' (Pierson 1989: 20). Instead, Maggi and Carolyn experienced 'rampant hetero-sexism and homo-hatred' (Neuger and Poling 1997: 165). This is a practice of discrimination that many gay people have experienced, and so it was one that we especially needed to 're-story' (Laird 1989: 439) within the group.

ALTERNATIVE STORIES OF THE PASTORAL CARE OF CHRISTIAN GAY WOMEN

Because Maggi and Carolyn did not want their children growing up believing that there was something wrong with their family, they felt that it was necessary to get up and walk out of the service mentioned above. In doing this, they were resisting the discourses that were prevalent in the church that morning. Halperin (1995: 30) suggests that 'we don't refute discourses, we resist them'. Maggie completed this resistance to the heterosexist discourse by emailing the minister later on during the week, and explaining their presence at church and their reasons for leaving during the middle of the sermon. She concluded her letter by saying that she 'cannot join a church where my kids will be indoctrinated into believing I am sinful'.

This story of resistance to the church being unsafe, was embellished in other ways too during our time together as a research and support group. Halperin (1995: 60) speaks of resistance not being negation, but being creative. Bernice spoke of her experience of the creativity of her home church when she described it as being a place that she came to because it was a 'circle of love'. This resonates with the way in which Williams describes community: 'discovering that there is a group in which there is real love' (cited in Patton 1992: 20). Patton believes that pastoral care is partly done through community (1992: 15), and so it is that I have come to believe that Bernice's positive experience of community at her church was a good experience of pastoral care for her.

Theresa spoke of 'how wonderful' the Catholic priest was when she confessed to being gay. She also spoke about how affirmed she felt when her priest prayed for 'gay couples in faithful relationships' along with other family prayers. This is an example of what Patton (1992: 28) calls 're-membering'. He says that 're-membering' is putting 'the body back together. The opposite of remember is not to forget, but to dis-member' (Patton 1992: 28). As gay people, like Theresa, were included back into the community of the church through this priest's prayers, they were remembered and effectively pastorally cared for.

Des shared that she felt it would be helpful for other people to experience the acceptance she had received in this research group. She spoke about how she had previously kept a distance to protect herself from the judgement of other people, and how she had realised that she now needed to let people into her life. She said that realising the fact that no one at her home church had ever condemned her, helped her to have the courage to allow people into her life. This realisation started to build trust into Des's life. McNeill (1994: 317) tells us that the 'spiritual struggle, then, for most gays and lesbians is to achieve trust'. As Des developed this trust, her resistance to the discourse of distancing herself from others was very creative. Together with her partner, she wrote two songs. Here is an excerpt from each:

Borderline
Here lie the valleys of my mind
And the heart of a faithful child
My soul was hidden from the unknowing crowd
Come and see me now
We'll explore never-ending horizons
And try not to look back
Cross over with me now
Take my hand

O'Neill and Ritter (1992: 210) tell us that one of the healing journeys that many gay people embark on is a journey 'from disconnectedness toward interrelatedness'. This seems to resonate with Des's journey, for the next song she sang to us was about how much she is yearning to find a spiritual home, and is considering returning to church:

Find your home
Only there will you be safe
Find your home
Only there will you be loved
Find your home
Only there will you be understood
Only there will you find what you've been looking for

Find your home
Only there will the clouds be blown away
Find your home
Only there will your soul fly to the sun
Find your home
Only there will your feet be on the ground
Only there will you feel that you can truly grow

If our churches can be experienced by gay people as a home for the heart, then our creative stand, resisting the discourse of church 'unsafeness', will have been everything we dreamed!

Maggi and Carolyn's resistance to the discriminatory practices of homophobia gave the research participants a way to begin to 're-story' their experiences of pastoral care, to include stories of love, of trust and of connectedness. Maggi and Carolyn's resistance to the heterosexism that they experienced when visiting the other church, by literally 'standing up' and walking out of the church, also became the spark around which the last and final strand of conversation, described in this research report, revolved.

TEXTS AND STANDING UP

Dominant Discourses Surrounding 'Standing Up' as Christian Gay Women

Once Maggi and Carolyn had shared their story of having walked out of the church service, many of the group's conversations from then on revolved around the question: 'What are your feelings about standing up?' I have been deeply challenged by Mel White's (1998) article *Bringing in the Beloved Community*. Previously a ghostwriter for many evangelical leaders, when his homosexual orientation became public knowledge, White set up a support centre for gay Christian people. In so doing, he hoped to gain some acceptance, if not justice, for gay Christians, but in a non-violent way. After some time he began to feel that he was not accomplishing that which he had hoped, and he was tired of constantly fighting against the evangelical homophobic discourses of the very people he used to write for. In his article, he spoke about the temptation to give up on trying to get people to see that 'anti-gay rhetoric sanctioned and led (directly and indirectly) to the suffering and death of God's lesbian and gay children'. But then he told the story of how he had received a letter in which he was told that he had 'broken a primary rule for doing justice non-violently. Giving up on my adversary was "an act of violence"' (White 1998: 2). I shared with the group how this article had challenged me to continue to 'stand up'. By this I meant not giving up on speaking about the need for Christian gay people to be accepted into every level of the life of the group.

As a group, we understood 'standing up' as being quite similar to the idea of 'coming out of the closet'. However, because in the church one is normally considered 'immoral' for being gay, 'coming out' is often not just self-disclosure, but is also, to some extent, necessarily a justification of gay orientation and practice. As a result, it is much easier for Christian gay people to give in to practices of silence about being gay in the church – as indeed some of the research participants, and as Mel White, were tempted to do. Most of the research participants began the research preferring to remain fairly quiet about their orientation at their home church. All of them had felt at least some disapproval from others that led to them thinking that it was better to simply remain silent.

Pixie felt that each of the group members needed to follow their own path with regard to standing up, because each person is different. Marshall (1994: 76) agrees with her, saying that it takes a 'great deal of courage' to stand against the 'hetero-sexism of church and academy which encourages silence and invisibility'. Marshall suggests that it is 'audacious for those within the safety of the academy or the institutional church to encourage lesbians and gays to name their pain publicly' (1994: 76). Theresa, who was very aware of the discourses of judgement that surround being gay, spoke of not wanting to alienate people by standing up and therefore forcing people to face the question of a justification of a Christian gay lifestyle. Des had her 'distance', which she used to prevent herself from being judged. If she did not get too close to people, she wouldn't have to face the tough questions that justifying her sexual identity would entail. Bernice, because she could not yet integrate the sexual and spiritual stories of her life for herself, was certainly not yet ready to justify herself to other possibly critical people. She felt that she did not yet have a story that she could stand up with, but that, when she did, she would. Maggi and Carolyn said that although they did not hide their sexual orientation, they did not parade it either. They hoped that people would get to know them, like them and only then find out that they were gay. In this way, they hoped to challenge people's homophobia, by providing it with a face that they (already) liked. This would be a necessary first step towards a justification of a Christian gay lifestyle for them. As we talked, however, the positions that each of the research participants initially held gradually developed into thinking about taking much stronger positions.

Alternative Stories of 'Standing Up' as Christian Gay Women

While all the women in the group had begun to take up a stance against 'silence', it was Maggi and Carolyn who had a different sort of resistance to the discourse of silence. They both stated categorically from the word go that they do not see themselves as being 'marginalised'. Because she now sees herself as an insider at her home church, Carolyn feels that the church must listen to her, and in fact even begin to make space for her, as she does for them. Des also felt that if people in the church could get to know her, then they would have to say 'Des is wrong', rather than 'being gay' is wrong, and this would be a way of getting them to think twice about the issue.

Bernice had attended a church service during which Carolyn had publicly shared her faith. She shared how seeing Carolyn physically stand up in the front of the church to share her testimony with the congregation had inspired her, just knowing that there was someone in the church who was both openly gay and a Christian. Theresa suggested that 'standing up' (or justifying a gay orientation) could be done powerfully in small ways, like when her priest had prayed for gay couples in faithful relationships along with other prayers for family life. Theresa spoke of how powerfully that re-categorisation of gay people, from being grouped with paedophiles to being grouped with families, had impacted on her own view of herself.

Maggi agreed with Theresa that it was the ministers who needed to be the ones doing the 'standing up'. She said that she thought ministers sometimes forget that they still have a very powerful voice, and that it needs to be used. McCall Tigert (1998: 137) tells us that just as a person who is disabled is not expected to build the ramp into church, so gay people should not have to defend their right to be part of any church community.

Carolyn spoke of her longing for there to be some place in the life of the church, perhaps a 'special-interest' gay cell group (although Maggi commented that she does not like what that has to say about marginalisation), or perhaps a published gay care-line, or 'gay issues' evenings where topics like this could be addressed. Des spoke of the need that her Mom had for a 'parents of a gay person' support group, and suggested the need for a gay teen support group. Bernice commented that, as a teacher, she was amazed by the freedom that teens had to identify themselves 'with the gay scene'.

She felt that if the church did not do something soon about its position on gay teens, then we would lose a lot of young people from the church. Carolyn said that being in this group had totally changed her. She said that she had moved 'inside of herself' from a place of 'complacency' to a place where she wants to evangelise people in the 'gay scene', and let them know that they are welcome, just as they are, at her home church! She also said that having children has changed this need in her to stand up, as she does not want them to be ashamed of her, and said: 'if we're ashamed of ourselves, then they'll be ashamed of me.'

The dangerous dichotomy between a love and preservation of self (exemplified by silence) and a love and preservation of others (exemplified by standing up) was thus breached during the group meetings. All of the women, but especially Carolyn, were able to start seeing that working with others is not losing oneself, but rather, 'first and foremost, it is to find a larger self' (Welch 1990: 162). And when that 'larger self' is found, then 'people are empowered to work for justice by their love for others and by the love that they receive from others' (Welch 1990: 165).

I was excited at the 'future stories' that these research participants have created together. Just as narratives always move to a climax, and then to a resolution, so 'human' stories must also be going somewhere and have a future dimension. When I ask myself the question, 'what is the future story of gay women in the church?' I am filled with hope, as I envision together with them communities of acceptance and care, where condemnation has been transformed into communion.

OUR LAST MEETING TOGETHER

At our last meeting together, we all had a chance to 'stand up' to the silence in the church that surrounds gay issues. I had invited the Bishop of our District to come and listen to the stories of the research participants. For me it was a standing up of 'voices speaking truth to power' (Heskins 2001: 187) as it was my public profession of where I stand on the issue to someone who has authority over my life. In that moment, I made the 'self a site for politicisation' (Hooks 1997: 534). Each of the women had a chance to read or sing the 'texts' which they had created which spoke of their views and their experience of being gay and being Christian. With these texts, we were able to integrate something of all that we had experienced during the four months of our being together.

At our last meeting, we were able to 'thicken' our positive, alternative experience of the church and pastoral care through our interactions with the Bishop. When he arrived, he laughingly remarked that he had 'been told to shut up and listen'. And that is really what he did. And when he had finished listening, he spoke about the proposal that would be going to Conference and that, although he had little hope of it being accepted by all ministers, it was an exciting document. He spoke of the years that the Methodist Church has been avoiding this issue, and of the need for the church to now face it squarely. And he spoke of his own determination that the church should be a place of love and acceptance. Then we prayed together, and, because 'rituals and celebrations mark significant steps in the journey away from a problem story to a new and preferred version of life' (Morgan 2000: 111), we had a celebratory tea with a heart-shaped 'Joy' cake. This was symbolic of the 'irrepressible joy' (Frost 1994) I described earlier as being a catalyst for authenticity, and of our joy in communal resistance (Welch 1999: 107). The Bishop stayed with us, and continued to listen to our informal stories.

Also at this last meeting, I provided each research participant with a rainbow bookmark (remembering that the rainbow is a gay symbol) with the text from Genesis 9: 16, where God gives the rainbow to Noah as a sign of God's everlasting covenant with all living creatures of every kind on the earth. In this way, I sought to symbolise for all of us the integration of our sexual and spiritual stories. Heskins (2001: 194) reminds us of the value of using symbol to retrieve a healing ministry.

It was the letters that I received after the last meeting that meant the most to me. I have already spoken about the letter I received from Theresa, in which she said: 'I am at the start of a great personal journey. I feel an increasing awareness of God's love for me, and this is almost too awesome to contemplate'. Later she said, 'in sharing your faith and joy of God's love you have given me a great gift'. Des wrote, in a note of thanks to me at the end of the research, 'What started out as your research has actually ended up as a re-awakening for us. Thank you for starting us on our spiritual journey again.' These alternative stories of a more intimate picture of God thrill me more than any other change my group has experienced. Earlier I spoke of my commitment to prayer as the natural work of spirituality. Walter Wink (1998: 181), the great activist, states that 'unprotected by prayer, our social activism runs the danger of becoming self-justifying good works'. I want neither to be involved in a group that is merely self-justifying, nor to be caught up in the 'counter ideology of some counter-Power' (Wink 1998: 181). It is when profound healing takes place in people's pictures of God, that people are transformed by God. 'We are not easily reduced to prayer' (Wink 1998: 180). But, when 'the spiritual is at the core of everything' then everything 'is therefore infinitely permeable to prayer' (Wink 1998: 184) and 'we may see ourselves – and maybe even the world – a little bit transformed' (Wink 1998: 200).

CONCLUSION

In May 2001, I was a delegate to the Highveld and Swaziland District Synod at which Bishop Peter Lee of the Anglican Church delivered a Bible Study on the Great Commission using Matthew 28: 18–20 and Acts 1: 6–7 as his texts. He urged us to encourage the church to do just three things. He said that as the church we had to 'look', we had to 'care', and then we needed to 'go'. He encouraged us all to really interrogate places of pain in our own and other communities. He reminded us that this would cause us to 'care', and that we would end up paying a price for this care, because we would end up going to stand in solidarity with those who are suffering. This research project has been a commitment of mine to understanding, to 'looking' as closely as I know how into what it is like for the research participants to be Christian and gay, and in the Methodist church. As Bishop Lee said it would, this looking has caused me to care even more deeply than I already did. I am now more deeply concerned than ever before that if we continue in our current position, the church will only succeed in trapping gay people into dishonest marriages, promiscuity, depression and suicide, or chase them from 'their mother', the church, forever. This 'caring' tells me that it is time for me to 'go'.

Since I was a little girl I longed to be a minister, and if I could not, well then, a minister's wife would do. Spirituality has been my closest companion for all of my life-journey so far. I have had another intimate companion on my journey, who joined me much later in my life – my sexuality. These two companions have, for the most part, been on good terms with each other, and as a result my journey together with them has been a very happy one. I can't imagine how difficult it would be for me if these two companions were to go into a contest with each other. I have experienced that the ways in which I have ordered my sexual life have signalled my highest priorities, my deepest sense of who I am, and who it is to whom I can be faithful and true.

Sadly, though, this research journey has shown me that for many people within the church, for one reason or another, these two companions are at loggerheads with one another. Many gay Christians feel, like Theresa, that they are a disappointment to God, even though God is at their centre. As I reach the end of this research process, I find myself standing in the place Wink (1999: 1) describes as 'rendered delicate towards ourselves and others'. The pain that I have encountered in the stories of the research participants, in the members of the same-sex discussion groups, as they struggle to understand a new way of doing Christian sexual ethics, and in the reading that I have done, has challenged me to live in a way that uses this knowledge respectfully. I truly believe that as a church we are all impoverished if we do not extend to all these holy sisters and brothers the church's support for their commitment to constant discipleship; I have been allowed into the most intimate places of all: the confluence of the sexual and spiritual lives of my co-researchers. As a fellow pilgrim, I have tried with all my capacity to listen respectfully within this sacred space, not only to each fellow traveller, but also to what it is that 'the spirit is saying to the churches' (Revelation 2: 7).

> *We stand, blessed, before this stupendous gift*
> *the mystery of human sexuality –*
> *awed, confused, and rendered delicate towards*
> *ourselves and others as we seek to listen closely to the*
> *new things the spirit is saying to the churches*
> (Wink 1999: 1)

BIBLIOGRAPHY

Brash, A 1995. *Facing Our Differences: The Churches and Their Gay and Lesbian Members*. New York: World Council of Churches.

Corn, A 1995. What is the Sexual Orientation of a Christian? in Boundry, B (ed), *Wrestling with the Angel: Faith and Religion in the Lives of Gay Men*, 203–220. New York: Riverhead.

DEWCOM 2001. Christians and Same Sex Relationships. Paper presented at Methodist Church of Southern Africa Conference. Port Elizabeth.

DEWCOM 2003. The Methodist Church and Same Sex Relationships: Summary Statement of Discussion Paper. Paper presented at Methodist Church of Southern Africa Conference. Pretoria.

Empereur, J 1998. *Spiritual Direction and the Gay Person*. New York: Continuum.

Frost, R 2001. Graced, Gifted and Gay. *Dialog* 40: 33–39.

Gerkin, C 1991. *Prophetic Pastoral Practice: A Christian Vision of Life Together*. Nashville: Abingdon.

Halperin, D 1995. *Saint Foucault: Towards a Gay Hagiography*. Oxford: Oxford University Press.

Heskins, J 2001. *Unheard Voices*. London: Dartman, Longman & Todd

Ind, J 2003. *Memories of Bliss: God, Sex and Us*. London: SCM.

Isherwood, L & McEwan, D 1996. *An A to Z of Feminist Theology*. Sheffield: Sheffield Academic Press.

Laird, J 1989. Women and Stories: Restorying Women's Self-constructions, in McGoldrick, Anderson & Walsh 1989: 427–450.

Mc Call Tigert, L M 1996. *Coming Out While Staying In: Struggles and Celebration of Lesbians, Gays and Bisexuals in the Church*. Cleveland: United Church Press.

McClain-Taylor, M 1996. But isn't it a Sin? in Wink 1999: 74–85.

Marshall, J 1994. Pastoral Theology and Lesbian/Gay/Bisexual Experiences. *Journal of Pastoral Theology* 4: 73–79.

Morgan, A 2000. *What is Narrative Therapy? An Easy-to-Read Introduction*. Adelaide: Dulwich Centre Publications.

O'Neill, C & Ritter, K 1992. *Coming Out Within: Stages of Spiritual Awakening for Lesbians and Gay Men*. New York: Harper.

Patton, J 1992. *Pastoral Care in Context: An Introduction to Pastoral Care.* Louisville: Westminster John Knox Press.

Peterson, E 1993b. *Working the Angles: The Shape of Pastoral Integrity.* Grand Rapids: Eerdmans

Walsch, N D 1997. *Conversations with God.* London: Hodder and Stoughton.

Welch, S 1990. *A Feminine Ethic of Risk.* Minneapolis: Fortress Press.

White, Mel 1998. Bringing in the Beloved Community. www.theotherside.org/archive/ jan-feb98/white. Retrieved on 16/08/2002.

White, M & Epston, D 1990. *Narrative Means to Therapeutic Ends.* New York: Norton.

Wink, W (ed) 1999. *Homosexuality and Christian Faith: Questions of Conscience for the Churches.* Minneapolis: Augsburg Fortress.

Wylie, M.S. 1994. Panning for gold. *Family Therapy Networker* 18 (6): 40–48.

THE USE OF RAPE IN THE BIBLE AS A MILITARY METAPHOR

PMS Matsepe

ABSTRACT

Media pages in South Africa in the past twelve months have been littered with reports containing the harrowing details of girl children being brutally raped and murdered. In many cases men rape and kill girls to settle scores with the girls' parents – either the father who has wronged the perpetrator or the mother who has decided to end a relationship with the perpetrator. While even babies and infants are raped, teenage girls are often gang-raped and murdered. Some are 'lucky' to survive the rapes and tell their stories. These incidents, coupled with the high pregnancy rate at secondary schools, paint a picture of girl children under siege and a nation that seemingly throws its hands up in resignation. The story found in Judges 19, where a young woman is gang-raped, murdered and dismembered, provides a chilling reminder of the way society can tolerate the gang-rape of young women. In the *Yizo-Yizo* drama series on SABC TV, a schoolgirl was raped and there was no public outcry. But when a male actor was raped in jail by a prison inmate, there was a huge wave of protest which extended even to parliament. We seem to be able to live with the rape of a girl, but we cannot accept the rape of a boy.

INTRODUCTION

Feminist Biblical scholars, Athalya Brenner (1995), T.D.Setel (1985), Rachel Magdalene (1995), and Pamela Gordon and Harold Washington (1995), have decried the use of rape as a military metaphor in the Bible, particularly in the prophetic corpus of the Bible. They refer to texts in which cities are frequently personified as women and God is characterised as a male who regularly threatens 'in judgement, to rape or otherwise sexually abuse the cities of Israel, Judah and their neighbours' (Magdalene 1995: 327). Gordon and Washington note that the context of these texts is usually associated with military disaster where women are often the victims of such offences (1995: 308). One such text is Nahum 3: 5f: 'Behold, I am against you [the city of Nineveh], says the Lord of hosts, and will lift up your skirts over your face; and I will let nations look on your shame. I will throw filth at you and treat you with contempt, and make you a spectacle'.

The use of sexual language and imagery by the prophetic books to describe military conquest has prompted Setel and others to call for the abandonment of these texts, which they refer to as 'pornographic' (1985: 86). Gordon and Washington draw on the memoirs of the Vietnam War era, which highlight 'the soldiers' habit of describing their attacks on land, villages and people with graphic language of the violation of the female body' (1985: 309). I wish to argue that this use of language is linked directly with the actual sexual abuse of women, because it makes it normal and acceptable to abuse women. A further reason is that the pornographic metaphor is not confined to the Biblical world, but is still in use in many African communities today.

DEFINITION

It is important to provide some working definition of pornography and rape. Noting that pornography has contributed to the power relationships of patriarchal society, Gordon and Washington define it as 'representation that objectifies women, exploits sexuality as a means of domination, expresses hostility and imputes defilement' (1985: 311). Rape, in legal terms in South Africa, is defined as the act of sexual penetration of a woman by a man without the woman's consent. The law goes on to define 'statutory rape' as sexual intercourse between an adult man and a girl under sixteen years of age, even if the girl has given consent. This definition of rape carries the possibility of making it a punishable offence for a man to have sexual intercourse with his lawfully married wife against her will. Of course, husbands have met this section of the legal definition of rape with consternation and protest. For them it is acceptable to have sex with their wives even against their will. Some Biblical scholars have argued that it is unfair to judge ancient texts by modern standards. I wish to differ. While it may be helpful to understand what these texts meant to their original audiences, we have to accept that these texts speak to us, the present readers, in our context.

Our interpretation will be informed to a large extent by our context, our world view and our life experience. I contend that the use of rape and sexual violence as a war metaphor, both in the Biblical world and ours, has contributed, and continues to contribute, to sexual violence against women and girls in violent conflict situations. Susan Niditch (1993: 107) observes that the motif of stealing or raping the women of another group is a very ancient one in traditional narrative and speaks to 'one of the most basic dilemmas in human social relations – namely how to steer the proper course between endogamy and exogamy'.

I now wish to provide evidence of how sexual violence is accepted as a normal war strategy in our world, in Africa and in South Africa. In her comment entitled *Rape as a weapon of war rips the social fabric*, Janine Moolman points out that thousands of women in the Congo are suffering from 'vaginal fistula – ruptured vaginal tissue as a result of brutal rape' in the war-ravaged country (The Star, 17 November 2003). She asserts that violent conflicts in the Democratic Republic of the Congo (DRC), Rwanda,

Burundi, Croatia and Yugoslavia have all been marked by sexual assault and the systematic rape of women and girls. I could add that in South Africa, during the state-sponsored political violence in African communities, it was common for the belligerents (mainly apartheid-supported hostel inmates) to abduct girls from the liberation movement-supported townships and to hold them as sex slaves. Moolman laments that the fact that the 'destruction of the vagina' is recorded as a 'crime of combat' by doctors in itself speaks about the normalisation of rape as a tactic of war (*The Star*, 17 November 2003).

In trying to explain why women's bodies have become sites of struggle, Moolman argues that the recognition that women are traditionally the ones who maintain communities and keep families together is what makes them prime targets. She asks, rhetorically, 'what better way to hurt the enemy than to destroy the fragile social stability of their communities?' (*The Star*, 17 November 2003). Using rape as a weapon of war is a deliberate attempt to undermine the 'enemy'. The large-scale rape of women is an attack on the social fibre, and cultural and traditional integrity of 'enemy' communities.

Moolman describes in chilling detail the perversity in the brutal acts carried out in war-ravaged countries: whole communities are made to watch as women and girls they know are raped in public; boys and young men are forced to rape family members and older women in the communities in which they live; and women and girls are coerced to become 'wives' to those who rape them. This trauma naturally makes it impossible for women, even after the war is over, to come to terms with their experiences and to rebuild their lives. As Moolman rightly asks: 'How does one return to normality when one sees one's rapist in the eyes of one's own son/brother/husband? Or if the child borne by one's wife/sister/daughter is that of the enemy?' (*The Star*, 17 November 2003).

THE CONNECTION

I contend that the above proves the danger to women and girls caused by the metaphorical use in war of rape and pornography. The metaphor, as Gordon and Washington observe, 'is masculinist language: it formulates and promotes an unchallenged masculine authority that sanctions both violent sexual acts and the mayhem of warfare' (1985: 323). I concur with them that women and girls cannot be safe in the environment created by such rhetoric, since they are allotted the role of passive victims while men and boys are expected to pursue with enthusiasm sexual domination, war and other violent conflicts. This, I argue, provides the background against which to read texts such as Isaiah 3: 17–26; 47: 1–4; Jeremiah 13: 22–26; Ezekiel 16: 35–39; 23: 9–10, 26–29; Hosea 2: 4–5, 11–12 (verses 15ff are counter-text); Nahum 2: 7–8; 3: 5,13 and Zechariah 14: 2. It also serves to justify the labelling of these texts as 'hidden texts of terror'. Judges 19 as 'a hidden text of terror' is one of the contextual Bible study topics I have conducted as part of my research.

There are twenty girl learners in the Bible study research group. For the sake of practicality, I have focused on teenage girls who are in secondary school. I acknowledge that primary school girls (and even infants) are also victims of molestation, but at that age they can hardly make any meaningful contribution to the Bible studies. Therefore, although my research statistics include all girl learner victims, the Bible studies have only featured teenage girls in secondary school.

I have taken into consideration the most common types of abuse against women and girl learners that plague our nation. Chief among them is sexual violence, including the rape of girl learners. Reports abound of girl learners being raped at schools, especially on school excursions. Rape is carried out by either the boy learners or male teachers. Not only are girls raped at schools, but they have become sitting ducks in the community for men who are motivated by the myth that having sex with a virgin is a cure for HIV/AIDS. In the worst cases the girls are brutally gang-raped. Recent events that have made newspaper headlines make for horror reading. The stories of fourteen-year-old Thato Mokoena, who was gang-raped and murdered, and the two Mbhele teenage sisters, who suffered the same fate, are just two of the many reported cases of sexual assault on girl children in South Africa, particularly on girl learners. It is for this reason that I have chosen Judges 19, a story of gang-rape and murder.

THE CONTEXT OF JUDGES AND OUR CONTEXT

The book of Judges is set within a patriarchal system that granted privileges and rights 'according to gender and societal rank' (Jones-Warsaw 1993: 172). Men monopolised power and privilege due to wealth, age, birth order, and clan and tribal affiliation. The rights and privileges of women were derived from their relation to their father and his status, then the husband and, in widowhood, the sons (1993: 173). Jones-Warsaw points out that female sexuality was considered 'a valuable asset, protected and transferred from father to husband ... [and] virginity became a prized status among unmarried women, and contributed to their marriageability' (1993: 173).

Interestingly, many girls in Gauteng townships do not have their prized virginity status intact. The alarmingly high rates of pregnancy in township schools, and the long queues of teenaged girls at the banks at month-ends collecting social grants for their children, bears testimony to the sad reality that girl learners are violated by adult men and fellow boy learners alike. Reading Judges 19 with girl learners can be both depressing and liberating, as the Bible study review will show later.

Joseph R Jeter Jr summarises the text of Judges 19 in a highly emotive manner (Jeter Jr 2003: 134). Let me paraphrase his exposition and try to draw the reader into the world of the text some three thousand years ago. The reader is invited to have the following picture: suppose this unnamed woman were your daughter. She grew up gracefully, a lively and energetic child, and matured into womanhood. When the Levite man came to propose marriage, you graciously released your daughter to him, even though she would be a secondary wife. After all, the man must have been impressive and able to pay a handsome lobola.

Some time later you are shocked to find your daughter back on your doorstep, weeping and dejected. She tells you that the Levite physically abused her until she could not take it any more, and so she finally decided to return to the only safe place she knows: the home of her childhood, the home of her parents. You are obviously distressed that she has been beaten, but you also know that conventional wisdom declares that when women are beaten by their husbands, it must be because the woman deserved it. Furthermore, what worries you is the possibility that the Levite could come back at any time to reclaim his lobola, or part thereof, and you know full well that you have already spent it on some projects that would greatly increase your wealth and status in the community. So you decide to tell your daughter that she may enter your house, but as one who belongs to her husband, and that she has no right to be here without him. All this time you ponder on what your daughter could have done to cause you such embarrassment and whether the Levite will want his money back.

While you are still brooding over the above questions, the Levite shows up four months later. His expression seems to suggest that the break-up was just a result of a minor misunderstanding. So you welcome him warmly, and wine and dine him for some days before sending your daughter back with him with strict instructions to be humble and submissive, to do anything he demands of her. As they leave, the Levite riding the donkey with your daughter following, she turns back and looks at you. It does not occur to you that this may be the last time you will ever see her face. The look of resignation on her face leaves you feeling uneasy. Not long thereafter, you see a crowd coming down the street towards your house, following a man who is carrying a parcel in his arms. When they congregate at your door, the man begins to tell a story, but, before he concludes, you already know what has happened. The memories haunt you. The messenger tells how the Levite and your daughter had stopped for the night in Gibeah, hosted by an old man. A group of Benjamite rascals sought to attack the Levite, but the old man, in a bid to protect his male guest, offered the men his virgin daughter and the Levite's wife. When the men would not listen, the Levite took his wife and threw her outside to them, 'and they raped her and abused her throughout the night, and at dawn they let her go' (19: 25). After they finally tossed your daughter aside like a bag of dirty laundry, she managed to crawl some distance before reaching the door of the house where the Levite was staying, where she collapsed and died. The Levite had not told the messenger that your daughter was thrown to the mob to protect him not from murder, but from homosexual rape – since that is a 'disgraceful thing' (19: 23b) which would have dishonoured him. Neither did the Levite say that after your daughter had been thrown to the beasts, he went to bed, and in the morning, when he found your daughter at the doorstep, all he could say was 'Get up; let's go', (19: 28) rather than find out how was she doing. The messenger concludes his story by saying that, when the Levite got home, he cut your daughter into twelve pieces and sent them to all the areas of Israel, asking for help to have his honour restored. When the messenger unwraps the parcel, which holds a limb of your daughter, and lays it across the threshold, your worst fears have been confirmed. Your daughter has finally come home, even though just a piece of her. The gathered crowd murmurs vengeance and vows to help the Levite get his honour restored. No one seems interested in comforting you over the loss of your daughter, let alone the pain of not being able to give her a decent burial (Jeter Jr 2003: 134–5).

Any reader of this story naturally shudders at the abuse, rape, murder and dismemberment of this unnamed woman. Jeter says, sarcastically, 'Thank goodness this story is three thousand years old and not contemporary. Thank goodness we do not do this kind of thing any more, do we?' (2003: 136). Of course the reality is quite the opposite, as the scourge of rape and murder of girl children remains rampant in South African society.

Yet, recourse to the Bible seems to provide cold comfort as Magdalene observes: 'The first piece of property in the development of 'the house of the father' was a woman' (1995: 337). This is shown repeatedly in the writings of ancient Israel. In Exodus 20: 17 and Deuteronomy 5: 21 a wife is listed among the property of a man's house. In the former, she is listed as the first piece of property, and in the latter she is listed second after the house. Moreover, in the Old Testament we see the taking of brides as a way of asserting military power over conquered males. For example, a virgin captive who has been raped can be taken as a wife and be divorced, but not sold into slavery; yet the relationship began with a rape (Deuteronomy 21: 10–24). In such an environment, Magdalene asserts, a woman could neither consent to the sex act nor refuse it based on her understanding of bodily integrity (1995: 337). Instead, according to the laws in the books of Leviticus, Numbers, Deuteronomy and the narratives of Genesis, Judges and 2 Samuel, rape was the sexual violation of one man's property by another man: 'It was the theft from the father of the financially valuable virginity of his daughter. It was the theft from the husband of the economically valuable and exclusive right to pleasure and reproduction lodged in his wife' (1995: 337). Rape was therefore the means by which one group of men demonstrated their control of or dominance over another group of men by forced sexual access to the human female property of the weak (1993: 337). Brownmiller concurs that in 'war the body of a raped woman becomes a ceremonial battlefield, a parade ground for the victor's trooping of the colours. The act played out upon her is a message passed between men – vivid proof of victory for one and defeat for the other' (1975: 147).

It is against this background that the book of Judges is a selected text of the research.

BIBLIOGRAPHY

Brownmiller, S 1975. *Against Our Will: Men, Women and Rape*. New York: Simon & Schuster

Brenner, A (ed) 1995. *A Feminist Companion to the Latter Prophets*. Sheffield: Sheffield Academic Press

Gordon, P & Washington, H C 1995. Rape as a Military Metaphor in the Hebrew Bible, in *A Feminist Companion to the Latter Prophets,* Brenner, A (ed). Sheffield: Sheffield Academic Press

Jeter, J R Jr 2003. *Preaching Judges*. Saint Louis: Chalice Press

Jones-Warsaw, K 1993. Toward a Womanist Hermeneutic: A Reading of Judges 19–21, in *A Feminist Companion to Judges,* Brenner, A (ed)

Magdalene, R F 1995. Ancient Near Eastern Treaty-Curser and the Ultimate Texts of Terror: A Study of the Language of Divine Sexual Abuse in the Prophetic Corpus, in *A Feminist Companion to the Latter Prophets*, Brenner, A (ed). Sheffield: Sheffield Academic Press

Moolman, J. The Star, 17 November 2003. Johannesburg

Niditch, S 1993. *War in the Hebrew Bible: A Study in the Ethics of Violence*. Oxford: Oxford University Press

Setel, T D 1985. Prophets and Pornography: Female Sexual Imagery in Hosea, in *Feminist Interpretations of the Bible*, Russel, F M (ed). Oxford: Basil Blackwell

WHAT ABOUT AFFIRMATIVE ACTION FOR THEOLOGICAL APPLICATION?

Kevin Light

Here I make a case for giving special emphasis to experience *as the starting place and end point of theology. As an illustration of the need for this I explore the issue of same-sex unions from a phenomenological perspective in terms of the MCSA within its broad South African context.*

INTRODUCTION

Affirmative Action in South African politics, commerce and educational institutions is born out of the recognition that the injustices of the past have a current effect on the contribution of previously disadvantaged people. It is thus necessary to focus deliberately on the development of such people so that their participation in the collective might be enhanced and the whole of South Africa be enriched.

In similar vein, I would like to call for Affirmative Action for Theological Application. It has been disadvantaged, oppressed, and not given equal expression in the theological world where theories, writings and debates have dominated the stage. I call for a 'quota system' for Theological Application. In my opinion, for the foreseeable future, at least, Application should receive the first and best of our energy. It is how we should measure the skilfulness of our theology. Viva the Application of Theology, Viva! Down with Theological writings that, at best, merely suggest how Application might be considered, down! Viva the Applied, Practical, the Real, the Everyday, the Ordinary, Viva!

Where do you think God lives? It is a basic question, perhaps, and it is also a hugely important one. Gold and Perlman believe it to be so central that they explore it in their so-called children's book which is endorsed by Protestant, Catholic, Jewish and Buddhist leaders. So while the question might appear to be frivolous, it is universal in its significance.

The little girl in Gold and Perlman's book arrives at the discovery that, *inter alia*, 'God lives in all people here on the earth; that's why we all shine from the day of our birth.' (Gold and Perlman 2001: 20)

This insight echoes that wonderful verse found in Revelation 21: 3:

> And I heard a loud voice from the throne saying, 'Now the dwelling of God is with men, and he will live with them. They will be his people, and God himself will be with them and be their God.'

But what of the mystery, the transcendence of God? Exactly! What is it to us without an encounter, an experience of it? The burning bush, the fleece wet one day and dry the next, the sun standing still, the sweating blood in the Garden of Gethsemane, the empty tomb ... none of these experiences reduce the transcendence of God; they define it. It is the application of God to the experienced lives of people that causes them to change direction.

In his wonderfully clever novel *Life of Pi*, Yann Martel tells, in part, the story of a young man's encounter with Hinduism, Christianity and Islam. I regard it as a great comparative religious study because it focuses on how they are each experienced, and that by an adventurous fourteen year old child.

> This Son ... who goes hungry, who suffers from thirst, who gets tired, who is sad, who is anxious, who is heckled and harassed, who has to put up with followers who don't get it and oppo-

nents who don't respect Him – what kind of a god is that? It's a god on too human a scale, that's what ... This Son is a god who spent most of His time telling stories, *talking*. This Son is a god who walked, a pedestrian god – and in a hot place, at that – with a stride like any human stride, the sandal reaching just above the rocks along the way; and when He splurged on transportation, it was a regular donkey. This Son is a god who died in three hours, with moans, gasps and laments. What kind of a god is that? ... I'll stick to my Krishna, thank you very much. I find his divinity utterly compelling. You can keep your sweaty, chatty Son to yourself ...

Every day I burned with greater indignation against Him, found more flaws to Him ... I couldn't get Him out of my head. Still can't. (Martel 2002: 55ff)

It is the humanity of Jesus that someone like Piscine finds so compelling. In previous encounters he had come to understand issues of transcendence and divinity as they relate to God. But what is new, unique and ultimately occupies his consciousness and conscience is that Jesus is so tangible in human experience.

A colleague of mine once shared with me how each week he would prepare his sermon knowing that he'd better give careful attention to the application component thereof. He knew that it did not matter how deliberate his exegesis of scripture, how brilliantly reasoned his argument or how systematic his journey through the traditions of the church, if his application of it all to the lives of his hearers was not both relevant and practical, if it didn't come out of the current experience of his hearers' context, and go back there, he would be held to account later. No matter what, at the end of it all, my colleague's wife would be ready to ask her revealing question on the way home: 'That was very clever but, So What?'

Our theology is an empty vessel and a clanging cymbal unless it is incarnational, relational and experiential. Here and now. Stories, theories and traditions of the burning bush, the schizophrenically damp fleece, the stationary sun, the God who can cope with the turmoil of Gethsemane, the empty tomb ... are not enough. They weren't then, and they aren't now. No matter how many layers of redaction and theological dissertation-ing have happened. Like each of the people in those very stories, we long for, need, the God who lives here, now, for real. If it doesn't start and end with this world, it feels like a theological sales job. But I don't want to visit in other people's experiences of God. I want shares!

Bishop John Spong says that one of the central crises facing faith today is the question 'Did it really happen?' In his book, *Liberating the Gospels*, he traces the ways in which it has become increasingly difficult to answer a quick and unequivocal 'Yes!' He shows how, through the contributions of Copernicus, Galileo, Newton, Darwin, Freud and Einstein, 'The ability of a modern person to continue to view the Bible literally had all but disappeared.' (Spong 1996: 12)

I would like to highlight not so much the contribution of Galileo, but Spong's description of the treatment of this remarkably creative thinker by the Christian Church. His thinking about the earth's place and movement in the universe led him to question Scripture, reason and tradition as they had been known and used up to that point. In short, Galileo was condemned and given the choice between his discovered reality and his life. He chose life. The interpretation of Scripture, careful reasoning until that point and the established tradition of the Church, triumphed over the scientific experience of one man – for 350 years, that is, until 1991 when the Vatican finally 'admitted that Galileo had been correct and the Church and the Bible had been wrong ... By that time Galileo hardly cared, and the credibility of the Church was as poorly served by that arrogant confession as it had been by its original closed-minded ignorance.' (Spong 1996: 7)

I feel more sorry for the Church in this story than I do for Galileo. He only gave up admitting his own reality in order to preserve his life. The Church, on the other hand, gave up discovering life in order to try to save its reality. As Spong says, 'no external authority can ultimately repress truth.' (Spong 1996: 7) And I would add, especially not the lived truth of human experience.

Coming back to Bishop Spong's question, 'Did it really happen?' he says that his 'quest for truth [has been] delivered from a yes-or-no approach to the things of the spirit' and goes on to devote the rest of his excellent book to exploring the Gospels as 'Jewish attempts to interpret in a Jewish way the life of a Jewish man in whom the transcendence of God was believed to have been experienced in a fresh and powerful encounter.' (Spong 1996: 20) I am struck by how 'here and now, applicable to me and us' understanding of the Gospels is. Will we practice the Gospel more skilfully when we repeat its content or its method?

I think that Spong's line of reasoning offers us a more important question than 'Did it really happen?' and that is, 'What *is* happening?'

'What is happening to me, to us, here, now?' This is the big 'So What?' question my colleague's wife kept asking and I regard it as the ultimate test for any theology. What difference does it make? Does it have handles that are within the reach of its hearers and connected to the stuff of their lives? Does it help, I mean really help, practically help, ordinary people to overcome fear and grief, live with hope and make sense of their world? Is it pedestrian, sweaty, regular, human?

So let me ask you where your default place of comfort lies: are you a Biblicist, a Rationalist, a Traditionalist or an Experientialist? Yes, yes, I know that the correct answer is that our Wesleyan theology is a pot with all four legs and that we must balance each one with the others, but where does your bias lie? Which leg is thicker on your doctrinal dish?

You'll have realised by now that it's the 'warmed heart' that gets me. I admit that more than Luther's preface to the Epistle to the Romans, much more than the time in Oxford and the boat trip to America, and infinitely more than the Methodist traditions that have followed it, it is Wesley's *experience* that grabs me. As Bewes puts it, 'A flame was lit that evening in London,' and he goes on to quote from Wesley's journal: 'I felt my heart strangely warmed. I felt I did trust in Christ, Christ alone for salvation: and an assurance was given me, that He had taken away *my* sins, even mine, and saved *me* from the law of sin and death.' (Bewes 1986: 11)

John Wesley *felt* it. He didn't read it, nor think it through, nor inherit it – he felt it for himself. And it was that encounter, that experience, that changed him. And changed his friends. And his country. Not because he told them about it, but because they came to experience it too. And that happened because Wesley met them where they were in their time and space. He learned how to do that because he knew from personal experience that it is experience that counts. We must tell Wesley's story by learning his skill of Application, not by getting cleverer at reciting it. I believe that we do Mr. Wesley no honour by reminiscing about his story at the expense of replicating his radical relevance.

The Celtic church too was so focused on engaging its surrounding environment that mission was its reason for being. The Celtic Christians were more interested in perpetuating a climate of faith experienced than they were in preserving faith inherited.

> They were not trying to establish a church order on earth so much as expressing the essential unity of the cosmos ... Heaven was being brought to earth rather than the earth being accommodated to heaven. There was no reporting back to a single directing authority. Rather the impulse for mission was contained within the very self-replicating nature of the communities themselves. Founded in mission, engaging in mission, they continued to train missionaries wherever they were. (Robinson 2000: 177)

Can you imagine what might happen if the Methodist Church today prioritised mission at the expense of 'reporting back to a single directing authority'? If we liberated mission by trusting the experiential, and therefore essentially untidy, reality of faith?

So, which leg is thicker on your theological tray? Where does authority finally reside? Where does your spirit seek when you need to find a solution?

It happens for me in the forest and on the mountain, running hard, with the sun on my back and sweat on my chest. There She comes, like a bright Dove of Peace, reminding me that I am loved, even me! And then I remember a verse of scripture about how the wilderness wanderers were encountered on the desert road. And I think of the two disciples who were on the road to Emmaus when he asked them, 'What is it that you are talking about as you walk?' And then I'm reminded of the many journey theologies. And the throng of those who have encountered the Ground of our Being in nature throughout the history of Christianity. And Mr Wesley who was out there in the elements on his horse. But it comes back to where it started – for me, on this mountain, in this week, in this context, and how I will live because of this experience.

And sometimes it happens for me at a table, with food and friends. There is laughter and appreciation of the basic pleasures of colour and taste. And I suddenly realise that He is present. Laughing. Eating. And I feel deeply connected. And then the verses come back to me about how He sat at the table of this one or that and broke bread with them. And only then do I think of the theory of the Eucharistic Sacrament. But it comes back to where it started – to this table, in this family, facing these realities, and I am empowered to ask more carefully, to listen more deeply.

Theology must start and end with experience if it is to be theology at all. The very word 'incarnation' begs it. From the Latin *en carne*, meaning, 'in the meat', the basis of our theology about where God lives is that Jesus lives in us. Let us start and end with that reality.

Now, an issue that occupies much of our theology at this time, in this place, is that of same-sex unions. It has long been an issue for us.

I remember how I represented the Divinity Faculty in a public debate on the topic during human rights week while I was a student at Rhodes University more than 15 years ago. My debating team partner was human rights lawyer, Edwin Cameron. He went on to display incredible courage by disclosing his HIV-positive status to the Judicial Service Commission while being interviewed for a Constitutional Court Post.

But we in the Methodist Church of Southern Africa (MCSA), we debated the theology.

In 1996 South Africa passed into law one of the most amazing constitutions in human history. Section 9 entitled 'Equality' specifically includes sexual orientation because of the injustices gay and lesbian people have suffered in South Africa. This made South Africa the first country to enshrine gay rights in its constitution and thus provide all of its citizens with a society freer of discrimination. (http://www.acts.co.za/constitution)

The writing was undeniably on the wall but we in the MCSA, we debated the theology.

Case CCT 10/99 saw the High Court of South Africa extend the same immigration benefits previously afforded to 'spouses' to same-sex couples on the basis that to practice otherwise was an infringement of their dignity. That was back in 1999. (http://www.concourt.gov.za/text/rights/know/homosexual.html)

There were people reading the writing on the wall out loud, but we in the MCSA, we debated the theology.

The Constitutional Court ruled on 1 December 2005 that same-sex marriage was to be made legal by parliament within one year. (http://en.wikipedia.org/wiki/Same-sex_marriage_in_South_Africa)

There were planning meetings taking place among the people sitting next to the writing on the wall, but we in the MCSA, we debated the theology.

On 30 November 2006 the Civil Unions Bill was enacted after having been passed by the South African Parliament earlier that month. (http://en.wikipedia.org/wiki/Same-sex_marriage_in_South_Africa)

There were weddings at the wall, but we in the MCSA, we debated the theology.

As recently as September 2007 the MCSA Conference resolved that 'any decision and subsequent action on the issue of civil unions between same-sex partners must await the outcome of the on-going process of engagement as specified by Conference 2005' (Yearbook 2006: 8.3, 75) and, in the interim, 'expects Methodist ministers to continue to offer pastoral care to homosexual individuals' (Yearbook 2007: 82).

Some tried to have that final word 'individuals' replaced with the word 'couples' – and failed. Even if you didn't know that, the specific emphasis on caring for individuals betrays the lack of practical relevance to the issue of same-sex loving. The 'on-going process' is exactly that, 'on-going'. It has been going on for years, has no clear milestones to ensure progress and has no *terminus ad quem*.

We in the MCSA, we debate the theology still!

This history reveals an appalling failure by the MCSA to lead effectively or plan strategically in the face of the obvious development of its context. More critically, however, it reveals just how oppressed Application is in the way we do theology. Scripture and homosexuality we have debated. Reasoning and homosexuality we have debated. Tradition and homosexuality we have debated. We have debated and we debate still. We will go on with our theological debate until the 'on-going process as specified' produces an 'outcome'.

But the on-the-ground human experience out of which the whole issue arose in the first place, and towards which its history was so clearly travelling, *that* our theology did not touch. In fact only very recently have we begun to speak about actually engaging with gay and lesbian Methodists. Speak about it! How long will it be before we actually do listen in any significant and practically effective way? I fear that by the time we get there, Galileo will hardly care and our integrity will be very weak indeed.

But in the meantime, there are people! Men-loving-men and women-loving-women who are people like the rest of us. And thus they are, like the rest of us, the very place where God lives, God's home. By God's choice. They experience that Presence in their lives and in their relationships and God can be experienced in them by those who have eyes to see and ears to hear. All of this time that we were debating the theology Jesus was at that wall. He lives with and in people. All people. That is why I am a Methodist. But I want to be one in Application first and last, with Scripture, Reason and Tradition serving this reality. I want to experience it for myself and celebrate its real effect in the lives of the people around me. All the people around me.

Let me leave you with these words of two homosexual Methodists:

> We want to be very clear: Oppression is the issue. We start at a place of God's baptismal mark on us – God's love and acceptance – and we move forward stirred by God's desire for everyone to be free from fear, free from hatred, free from hopelessness. Let not the Church be distracted by homophobic and heterosexist baggage. Let the Church be infused with liberation. (Bennett Alexander and Preston 1996: xix)

Viva, Theological Application, Viva!

BIBLIOGRAPHY

Bennett Alexander, M and Preston, J 1996. *We Were Baptised Too: Claiming God's Grace for Lesbians and Gays.* Kentucky: Westminster

Bewes, R (ed) 1981. *John Wesley's England.* New York: Seabury

Gold, A and Perlman, M J 2001. *Where Does God Live?* Skylight: Vermont

Martel, Y 2002. *Life of Pi.* Edinburgh: Canongate

Robinson, M 2000. *Rediscovering the Celts*. London: HarperCollins

Spong, J S 1996. *Liberating the Gospels: Reading the Bible with Jewish Eyes*. New York: HarperCollins

The Methodist Church of Southern Africa 2008. *2008 Yearbook*. Cape Town: Methodist Publishing House

MORE RED THAN GREEN

Dion Forster

A response to global warming and the environment from within the Methodist Church of Southern Africa.

INTRODUCTION[4]

Sadly, environmental concerns have not been high on the agenda of the Methodist Church of Southern Africa (MCSA). The same can be said of most of the mainline denominations in Southern Africa. Whilst the effects of global warming and the impact of environmental destruction have tangible effects on life in Southern Africa, there seem to be many more tangible and urgent issues causing the Churches to focus their efforts and energies elsewhere. These socio-economic issues have been labelled as 'red' concerns in this chapter. They will be considered in greater detail below.

This chapter will discuss why the churches in Southern Africa, and the MCSA in particular, have dealt less fully and strategically with 'green' concerns (a term used in this paper to refer collectively to environmental matters) and have chosen to focus more acutely upon 'red' concerns. It will also consider what the impact of a lack of care for the environment has upon the

---

4   This chapter was first published as an academic article in *The Epworth Review*. Vol. 35 No. 2, April 2008: 38–52. The referencing style therefore differs from the other chapters.

poorest of South Africa's population. The chapter ends with a number of pointers from African traditional religion and African Christian theology that can hold both 'red' and 'green' concerns in tension in order to help society work towards a theologically responsible approach to sustainable development.

'RED' MATTERS MORE THAN 'GREEN' – THAT'S THE WAY OF THE WORLD

The official policy of the MCSA contains only one resolution on the environment. It is to be found in paragraph 1.12 under the heading *The ecological crisis*:

> 1.12.1. Conference calls on all Methodists to co-operate with environmental organisations in their attempts to alert the public through a vigorous education campaign to the urgency and extent of the ecological problem and to actions that can be taken to deal with it, and to save our environment by reducing pollution, waste and destruction of the ozone layer. Conference requests Societies to monitor environmental issues in their areas and to publicise and oppose any moves which could displace people as has happened in Bushmanland where people were removed to allow the dumping of nuclear waste; and to embark on programmes of action to save our earth and report through Quarterly Meetings to SYNODs.[5]

Within the *Yearbook of the Methodist Church of Southern Africa* for 2007 (often referred to as the 'Minutes of Conference' in other Connexions) there are only two direct references to environmental issues. The most explicit of these is to be found in Chapter 3, a record of the statements adopted by the World Methodist Conference meetings in Seoul, South Korea, in 2006:

---

5   *Laws and Discipline of the Methodist Church of Southern Africa*, Cape Town: Methodist Publishing House, 2007, p. 227.

Goal 7: Ensure environmental sustainability
• Integrate the principles of sustainable development into country policies and programs; reverse loss of environmental resources
• Reduce by half the proportion of people without sustainable access to safe drinking water
• Achieve significant improvement in [the] lives of at least 100 million slum dwellers, by 2020.[6]

There is, however, no comment on this 'statement' from Seoul. Neither is it discussed or considered in any part of this official record of the Church for 2006.

The second reference to the environment and ecology is to be found in the address of the Presiding Bishop, the Rev Ivan Abrahams, to the Connexional Executive of the MCSA. In his address he affirms the bishops, ministers and laity of the MCSA for having 'listened carefully', and spoken 'authoritatively, and acted decisively to exercise a prophetic ministry by ... sharing the struggles of the landless for a sustainable livelihood' and 'caring for the environment'.[7]

Sadly these are the only two records on environmental concern in the official documents of the Church for 2006. The reality is, quite simply, that 'green' concerns to do not feature prominently on the agenda of the Methodist Church of Southern Africa.

Conversely, however, 'red' concerns receive a great deal of consideration and attention in both the Laws and Discipline and the Yearbook. By 'red' concerns I am referring to matters such as:

• Social structure and society (political issues, crime, violence, issues of gender, concerns over the worsening state of affairs in Zimbabwe, care for refugees etc.).

• Health (naturally HIV and AIDS is a significant concern in Southern Africa, the region that has the highest infection rate in the world.

---

6   *2007 Yearbook of the Methodist Church of Southern Africa*, Cape Town: Methodist Publishing House, 2007, p. 59.
7   *2007 Yearbook of the Methodist Church of Southern Africa*, Cape Town: Methodist Publishing House, 2007, p. 10.

Moreover, the South African Government's inability to deal decisively with this crisis has placed a great deal of responsibility upon religious and non-governmental organisations to offer care. So HIV and AIDS features prominently in the ministry reports and planning of the Church).

- Economic concerns (these include global economic concerns, such as western capitalism and its effects upon traditional African life, but it also includes the exploitation of the poor in Africa by international corporations which mine the wealth of poorer nations to enrich relatively few American and European stockholders. Naturally there are also concerns about corrupt leaders who exploit the poor in Southern Africa. In addition there are statements about job creation, black economic empowerment, affirmative action, and a host of other factors that churches should be supporting in order to address the large-scale poverty that is so prevalent in Southern African communities).

- Values and ideology (moral issues such as corruption [in relation to economics], sex outside of marriage [in relation to HIV and AIDS], same-sex relationships, culture and faith, and the erosion of traditional African values by western individualism and systems of capital gain).

It is not surprising that 'red' issues should receive much more attention and priority than 'green' issues in Southern Africa. There are two basic reasons for this emphasis. The first is the simple fact that globally 'green' issues are less of a priority than 'red' issues. The second is that the *immediate impact* of 'red' issues is more visible, and more powerfully felt, than the impact of 'green' issues. As mentioned above, this does not mean that 'green' issues are less important, but simply that 'red' issues are more urgent and pressing in the Southern African context.

'Red' issues first – a global trend

This phenomenon is not unique to Southern Africa. Urgent and tangible concerns, like hunger or disease, almost always seem to take priority over the important concerns of the environment. Whilst environmental concerns are extremely important and urgent for the survival of all humanity, they seem to be less tangible than the death of a child from hunger, or riots and political instability because of a widening gap between the rich and the poor.

Perspective is a powerful force in shaping the theology and mission of the Church. When one takes these powerful perceptions of urgency into account, and one mixes in the further complication of poorly developed 'popular' theology, the outcome can be quite disastrous. In Southern Africa the fastest growing churches are those that have been birthed from North American fundamentalist and prosperity movements.[8] Such church movements have addressed themselves almost exclusively to the most visible and pressing needs of people ('red' concerns). These include issues such as wealth creation in the face of poverty, miraculous healing in the presence of death, and building self-esteem and self-determination in the face of years of oppression under apartheid. It is little wonder that Southern Africans are flocking to 'faith tabernacles', 'miracle centres' and 'prosperity prophets'. Of course the growth of these independent faith movements has an impact upon the mainline denominations. Many Methodist ministers have begun to style themselves on the multi-million dollar North American ministries of persons such as Bishop T.D. Jakes. This is visible both in the content of their theology, and in their style of dress, mannerisms, and approach to liturgics. It must be kept in mind that 79 per cent of Southern Africans indicated in the 2001 national census that they were adherents of the Christian faith. Yet, while the Methodist Church of Southern Africa is still the largest mainline denomination in South Africa (with 9.3 per cent of the population indicating Methodist membership), it is an increasingly aging church. Young people are leaving Methodist churches in large numbers and moving across to these independent movements.[9] The Methodist

---

8   SA Government, Statistics SA, *The 2005/6 Christian Handbook*, WITS University Library, Johannesburg. 2005. These statistics are also available online at http://www. statssa.gov.za/census01/html/default.asp accessed 10 July 2007, 22h09. A theological critique of this data is available in J. Hendriks and J. Erasmus, 'Religion in South Africa: 2001, population census data. *Journal of Theology for Southern Africa*, Vol 121. 2005: pp. 88–111.
9   See the article by T. Stone, 'Building the Church', in *The Methodist Newspaper, Dimension*, (June 2007), 1 for further details.

churches that are growing are those that have done away with vestments, adopted a mix of African and contemporary North American worship music, emphasising healing from HIV, miracles of faith, praying for employment, and prosperity.[10]

Conversely, traditional mainline Methodism in Southern Africa, as with most mainline denominations in the region, shows significant dissonance between the official statements of the denomination and the real-world ministry of the local churches. The majority of local Methodist societies propagate an inherited approach to the Christian faith that is neither 'green', nor 'red'. The emphasis of the church is not so much on mission as it is on maintenance. These local congregations retain their older, loyal members through the familiarity of their worship services and their fellowship groups and uniformed organisations. However, mission (whether 'green' or 'red') is seldom a concern.

Kevin Light writes:

> The essence of the spirit of Methodist Mission that has become secondary to centralised, controlled institution is a vital connection to the rhythm of the life of the people around us. A defining commitment to serving *their* needs, *their* interests, *their* well-being. As my old dad used to say, 'The church is supposed to exist for the benefit of its non-members but it spends itself discussing itself.'[11]

Brian McLaren comments on such expressions of the Christian faith, writing of the growing discontent among younger, more ecologically aware, Christians:

> They share my belief that the versions of Christianity we inherited are largely flattened, watered down, tamed ... offering

---

10   See the blog post *A new religion in Soweto... God wants you to drive a 4X4...* http://www.spirituality.org.za/2007/10/new-religion-in-soweto-god-wants-you-to.html (accessed 19 December 2007, 10h13).

11   Kevin Light, 'What is Methodist Mission?' in *Methodism in Southern Africa: A celebration of Wesleyan mission* (Cape Town: Upper Room), (in the process of publication) W. Bentley, W and Author, * (eds.), 4.

us a ticket to heaven after death, but not challenging us to address the issues that threaten life on earth.[12]

The sad reality is that even secular society does not place a high premium
on 'green' concerns. When the question is asked, 'What are the biggest
problems in the world today?' the answers seldom include environmental
issues at the top of the list. I shall give just two prominent examples to
make this point.

Danish economist Bjorn Lomborg led a widely accepted study known as
the *Copenhagen Consensus*. It brought together experts from various fields
such as economics, science and sociology, to identify and consider what
the leading threats are in the world. i.e. what are the greatest dangers and
causes of suffering in the world? They prioritised these concerns in terms
of which items can be most effectively addressed based on what could be
realistically changed if sufficient funds could be raised.[13] Their list of the
top 10 global problems was:

1.   Hunger and malnutrition

2.   Climate change

3.   Conflicts

4.   Financial instability

5.   Water and sanitation

6.   Subsidies and trade barriers

7.   Population/migration

8.   Communicable diseases

9.   Education

10. Governance and corruption.

12   Brian McLaren, *Everything Must Change: Jesus, Global Crises, and a Revolution of
Hope* (Thomas Nelson, 2007), p. 3.
13   'Copenhagen Consensus Centre - CCC Home Page', http://www.
copenhagenconsensus.com/Default.aspx?ID=788 (accessed 22 December 2007 10h56)

Next, we have the eight top issues that the 191 members of the United Nations have pledged to address as 'Millennium Development Goals' by 2015.[14] They list the world's most pressing needs as:

1. Eradicate extreme poverty and hunger

2. Achieve universal primary education

3. Promote gender equality and empower women

4. Reduce child mortality

5. Improve maternal health

6. Combat HIV/AIDS, malaria and other diseases

7. Ensure environmental sustainability

8. Develop global partnerships for development.

It is clear from these two prominent bodies of research that 'red' concerns take precedence over 'green' concerns (with climate change featuring second in the *Copenhagen Consensus*, and environmental sustainability featuring seventh in the UN Millennium development goals).

Thus, there are both internal and external factors that have caused 'red' issues to feature more prominently than 'green' issues in the theology and mission of the Methodist Church of Southern Africa.

Sustainable development and the immediate concerns of Southern Africans

One of the great misconceptions that has led to the lesser concern for 'green' concerns in relation to 'red' is the false understanding that the two are not related. The reality is, of course, that many 'red' concerns (such as survival on the land) lead to 'green' concerns (such as deforestation and the extinction of certain species). The converse is also true: many 'green' concerns (such as flooding due to global warming) have led to an increase in 'red' concerns (loss of income, disease, the inability to farm, lack of access

14 'The UN Millennium Development Goals,' http://www.un.org/millenniumgoals/ (accessed 22 December 2007 11h05)

to clean drinking water, even starvation). Olivier writes:

> Humans, and the consequences of their ways of life – globally,
> significantly influenced by the values and attitudes engendered
> by Western industrialised life – have brought the world we live
> in to the brink of a global environmental catastrophe.[15]

In short, the demands that we make upon the environment to support life
are simply not sustainable in their current form. The imbalance between
'red' and 'green' priorities will eventually destroy both the Earth and all
that is living upon it. Hence, our current approach to life is 'unsustainable'
– what is required is an approach to living that balances both the 'red' concerns and the 'green' concerns.

> The challenge we face is one of changing our ways of life in such
> a way as to ensure an environmentally sustainable future.[16]

The term 'sustainable development' became popular in the 1980s. Since
then it has featured widely in academic literature and in debates on the
relationship between environmental concerns and the need for socio-economic development.

The 1996 Constitution of South Africa affirms that:

> Everyone has the right ... to have the environment protected for
> the benefit of present and future generations, through reason-
> able legislative and other measures that ... secure ecologically
> sustainable development and use of natural resources while
> promoting justifiable economic and social development.[17]

South Africa thus faces the challenge of developing itself economically and

---

15 David Olivier, 'Evangelical 'green': the challenge!' in *Looking Back, Moving Forward:
Reflections by South African Evangelicals.* (Johannesburg: TEASA, 2005), p. 124.
16 David Olivier, 'Evangelical 'green' the challenge!' in *Looking Back, Moving Forward:
Reflections by South African Evangelicals.* (Johannesburg: TEASA, 2005), p. 124.
17 The Constitution of South Africa: http://www.info.gov.za/documents/
constitution/index.htm (accessed 22 December 2007 11h32)

socially, without doing any further damage to the environment. This is an extremely arduous task when one considers that there are both internal factors (such as disease, racial struggles and high rates of unemployment) and external factors (such as trade restrictions, international debt and foreign disinvestment) to contend with. Woolard lists the following statistics to illustrate some of the most pressing 'red' concerns that need to be addressed in Southern Africa:

The extreme inequality evident in South Africa means that one sees destitution, hunger and overcrowding side-by-side with affluence.

- About 15% of adults are illiterate;

- 9.2% of children under 5 are malnourished;

- Life expectancy has fallen from 62 years in 1990 to 48 in 1999 as a consequence of AIDS;

- The infant mortality rate is 45 per 1,000 live births;

- The maternal mortality rate is 230 per 100,000 live births;

- Of the 44 million people in the country in 2000, about 8 million were surviving on less than the international dollar-a-day poverty line and 18 million were living on less than 2 dollars per day;

- 37% of households survive on less than R1000 per month (in 2002 Rands);

- 60% of the poor receive no social grants;

- Health expenditure is 7% of GNP, but less than half of this is public spending.[18]

This context is shaped, as pointed out above, by a history of colonialism and apartheid in its past, and global inequality, international exploitation and debt in its present. In reality the standard of living to which the Kingdom of God bears testimony will only be realised, in some measure, when there is greater justice, equity, freedom, and a vast improvement in the quality of life for the majority of South Africans.

---

18 Ingrid Woolard, 'An overview of poverty and inequality in South Africa', *Working Paper prepared for DFID (SA)*, July 2002 http://datafirst.cssr.uct.ac.za/resource/papers/woolard_2002.pdf (accessed 22 December 2007 12h05)

'GREEN' ISSUES IN SOUTHERN AFRICA

As mentioned above, the challenges to sustainable development within South Africa are numerous. However, South Africa has been blessed with an abundance of natural resources and there is a great hope that we shall be able to overcome the internal and external challenges to sustainable development through careful and disciplined management of the bounty of our nation. Regardless of this, there are some specific 'green' issues that will challenge this process. Among these ecological challenges to sustainable development one will find:

- Poor reproductive management. The increase in population growth continues to place a strain on our natural resources. For example, access to drinking water and arable land is a growing concern for many rural South Africans. While the demand for electricity in the cities of Southern Africa has increased to the extent that the national electricity provider cannot cope with the load. As a result, many South African cities have had to contend with extended power outages (referred to as 'load shedding') in order to prioritise the supply of electricity to industry.

- The need for increased productivity in agriculture has severely impacted the limited water resources of sub-Saharan Africa, and created problems with soil erosion and degradation of the nutrients in the soil.

- The Southern African economy has become largely dependent upon the exploitation of the declining mineral resources of the area (gold, platinum, coal and copper).

- Over-fishing continues to deplete coastal fish stocks.

- The apparent 'panacea of eco-tourism has proved to be full of pitfalls as a consequence of conflicts of interests between the needs of local marginalised communities, the imperatives of conserving bio-diversity and the interests of commercial tourist ventures'.[19]

---

19 David Field, 'The ethics of sustainable development.,' in *Questions About Life and Morality: Christian Ethics in South Africa Today*, eds. Louise Kretzschmar and Leonard Hull (Pretoria: Van Schaik, 1998), 221.

Field goes on to note that the 'ecological costs will be transformed into so-cial and economic costs if they are not addressed, and the environment debt of society as a whole is always paid most by those least able to do so – the poor'[20]. This reality has been borne out again and again in Southern Africa.

Sadly it is the poorest South Africans who live in the large 'informal set-tlements' that line the edges of the urban landscape. These 'squatter camps', as they are disparagingly referred to in the mainstream media, are usually made up of thousands of one bedroom dwellings constructed out of spare pieces of aluminium and plastic sheeting, wood and cardboard. They have no access to sanitation or drainage, and the little houses are seldom more than a few metres apart. In recent years the effects of global warming have been acutely felt by these informal settlers. Two examples of the effects of global warming on this group of the population have been, first, in colder and wetter winters people have had to rely on burning wood and paraf-fin to create warmth. Unfortunately, burning wood not only destroys the surrounding vegetation, but also creates air pollution. A further side-effect has been the death of scores of children, either through carbon monoxide poisoning as a result of poor ventilation indoors, or from burning to death when a shack catches alight from an exposed fire or candle.[21] The emergen-cy services are seldom able to reach individual shack fires since the shacks themselves are built so closely together that there is no space for emergency vehicles to reach the blaze. The second example relates to summer floods. Increased rainfall has resulted in many dwellers in informal settlements finding their homes flooded or destroyed, and lives have been lost in flash floods that have occurred with increasing frequency during the summer rainfall season.[22]

---

20 David Field, 'The ethics of sustainable development,' in *Questions About Life and Morality: Christian Ethics in South Africa Today*, eds. Louise Kretzschmar and Leonard Hull (Pretoria: Van Schaik, 1998), 221.

21 See the following internet article for one example of deaths caused by fire in informal settlements: 'Health 24 – Child, Content' http://www.health24.com/child/Safety/833-866,36859.asp (accessed 22 December 2007 10h35)

22 Please refer to the following bulletin that explains how the poor are impacted by torrential flooding in informal settlements 'Environmental Hazard management in informal settlements', http://www.buildnet.co.za/akani/2003/mar/environhazard.pdf (accessed 22 December 2007 10h37).

In developing nations, such as the six nations that make up the Connexion of the Methodist Church of Southern Africa, the Church is often the most pervasive and organised local community forum in the region. In fact, in many poorer communities the only formal buildings will be those belonging to the church. Moreover, the church is likely to have a minister stationed in a particular area (whether it be rural or urban) long before the government is able to fund aid workers.

The result is that the Church, and particularly South Africa's largest mainline denomination, the Methodist Church of Southern Africa, clearly has a significant role to play in managing this crisis. In the section that follows, some theological and practical suggestions will be made that may be of use to the Church as it seeks to support and help Southern African society to move ahead responsibly.

SOME STEPS TOWARDS A THEOLOGY OF 'RED' AND 'GREEN' IN SOUTHERN AFRICA

African Christian theology can provide some very useful insights for a theology that balances both the socio-economic 'red' concerns, and the environmental 'green' concerns of sustainable development. Naturally I shall not be able to deal with each of the points that follow in full, but these points could stimulate some thought and discussion among Methodists in Southern Africa, and even across the globe, in addressing the twin crises of 'red' and 'green' concerns in the region.

Ubuntu – the necessity of cosmic harmony from an African theological perspective

Before discussing specific points of Christian theology, it is worth considering some valuable insights that can be gleaned from African traditional religion and mythology. Within Southern African traditional culture there is a pervasive creation myth that offers a valuable insight into the African understanding of the structure of the cosmos. Setiloane records it as follows:

The first people came out of a hole in the ground. They came out together, men, with their wives and children and their animals: cattle, sheep, goats and dogs. They came from underneath the earth where, in the 'big abyss' which nothing can fill (*Mosima oo sa tlaleng*) they had always been living under the direction and sovereignty of *Modimo*. These people who emerged from the bowels of the earth did so under the direction of Modimo. They were led out of the hole by an agent of Modimo called *Loowe*. In comparison with them, this agent of Modimo was a giant. Even more striking was the fact that Loowe was a single-sided person, as if he had been sawn through the middle, with one arm, one foot and one eye. After Loowe had led the people to the surface of the earth he returned back into the *Mosima* to continue his abode there with Modimo and the other inhabitants.[23]

This myth conveys a number of significant theological concepts. Firstly, there is belief in a transcendent supreme being. This is a common feature in African Traditional Religion.[24] Secondly, there are, other than the persons living on earth (the created beings), a class of people who live with God: 'These inhabitants are known as *Batho ba Modimo* or, more commonly, *Badimo* – *the people of Modimo* – because they live with Modimo in the land of Modimo.'[25] Thus, there is a clear belief in the existence of a spiritual realm (here referred to as *Mosima* – the big abyss), where both Modimo and the *Batho ba Modimo* live. Lastly, for the purposes intended here, one can identify the importance of creation itself. It is interesting to note that, in this myth, humanity and the rest of creation come into being simultaneously (men, women, children and animals). This illustrates an under-

---

23   GM Setiloane, 'Towards a biocentric theology and ethic – via Africa', in *Faith science and African culture: African cosmology and Africa's contribution to science*, ed. CW Du Toit (Pretoria: Research Institute for Theology and Religion, 1998), 66.

24   SA Thorpe, *African traditional religions* (Pretoria: University of South Africa, 1991), 4.

25   G.M. Setiloane, 'Towards a biocentric theology and ethic – via Africa' in *Faith science and African culture: African cosmology and Africa's contribution to science* , ed. C.W. Du Toit (Pretoria: Research Institute for Theology and Religion, 1998), p. 66.

standing and expression of the need for respectful co-existence with living things in order to maintain the harmony of creation. For example, Ngubane[26] points out that for the individual Zulu, good health means much more than just a healthy body; health 'pertains to all that concerns the person including the perception of a harmonious, co-ordinated universe'. This is the goal towards which communities and individuals strive.

The occasion on which the above myth is often employed gives a further insight into the religious life of Africans. This myth is often celebrated as a ritual at the death of a person. Fond messages are sent with the dead at burial to the people in Mosima:

> 'Greet them for us', 'tell them to give us rain and prosperity', and the means for sustaining life are buried with the dead (such as seeds and working instruments) so that they can continue to provide for themselves in the land of Badimo.[27]

Thus Thorpe points out that:

> Health, balance, harmony, order, continuity are all key words. They not only describe a desirable present condition for individuals and the community, but also represent the goal towards which people constantly strive. This ideal needs to be maintained not only within the visible community but equally in relation to the invisible community, conceptualised as spiritual powers (e.g. the ancestors).[28]

The African traditional concept of *ubuntu* as harmony in the cosmos can be quite easily related to the 'eternal shalom' of the Old Testament, or the 'eschaton' of God's kingdom found in the New Testament. Having dis-

26 H Ngubane, *Body and mind in Zulu medicine: An ethnography for health and disease in Nyuswa-Zulu thought and practice.* (London: Academic Press, 1977), 28.
27 G.M. Setiloane, 'Towards a biocentric theology and ethic – via Africa' in *Faith science and African culture: African cosmology and Africa's contribution to science* , ed. C.W. Du Toit (Pretoria: Research Institute for Theology and Religion, 1998), p. 67.
28 SA Thorpe, *African Traditional Religions* (Pretoria: University of South Africa, 1991), p. 111.

cussed this overarching concept of *ubuntu,* I wish now to present a few further points from an African Christian theological perspective that relate to the balance between socio-economic 'red' concerns and environmental 'green' concerns.

The earth is the Lord's, and everything in it ...[29]

After the World Summit on Sustainable Development of 2002 a number of Churches and theologians from across Africa compiled some simple points to represent an African theological perspective on sustainable development in a global context.[30] These points are the skeleton upon which a responsible theology of sustainable development can be built. I shall briefly mention and discuss them below.

The guiding principle for this theology can be found within the context of both the creator and the creator's creation. This relationship of harmony, and the dependence of the creation upon the creator, is expressed very clearly in the following verses from Scripture:

> The earth is the LORD's and all that is in it, the world and those who live in it; for he has founded it on the seas, and established it on the rivers. Who shall ascend the hill of the LORD? And who shall stand in his holy place? Those who have clean hands and pure hearts, who do not lift up their souls to what is false, and do not swear deceitfully. They will receive blessing from the LORD, and vindication from the God of their salvation. (Psalm 24: 1–5)

---

29 For two very good examples of 'green' theologies from a Southern African perspective see: David Field, 'The ethics of sustainable development,' in *Questions About Life and Morality: Christian Ethics in South Africa Today,* eds. Louise Kretzschmar and Leonard Hull (Pretoria: Van Schaik, 1998) p. 219–30, and David Olivier, 'Evangelical 'green': the challenge!' in *Looking Back, Moving Forward: Reflections by South African Evangelicals.* (Johannesburg: TEASA, 2005), p. 119–47.

30 Statement adopted at the African Regional Consultation on Environment and Sustainability, held at Machakos, Kenya, 6–10 May 2002.

Based on this understanding of the universe, the theologians developed the following guiding statement: In the household of God (*oikos*) the management of the house (economy) has to be based on the logic of the house (ecology).

Firstly, it was affirmed that there is a need for repentance, since it is clear that in Africa, and in many other parts of the world, the earth no longer belongs to God. Rather, it has become the property of 'Governors ... who control the earth's resources ... for their own benefit'. These include 'Governors' such as political rulers, nation states, institutions such as the World Bank, the International Monetary Fund, the World Trade Organisation, developers who do not develop in the interest of the poor, and the most affluent 20 per cent of the world's population.[31] In this regard we would do well to heed the words of Jesus, 'the meek shall inherit the earth' (Matt. 5: 1-5).

Secondly, the matter of 'ownership' of, and 'stewardship' of, the earth and the earth's resources is addressed. It is clear that the earth and all of its resources are a gift from God for the sustenance and enrichment of all people's lives. Thus, there is a greater need for generosity, sharing, and participation in decision-making processes.

Thirdly, it is necessary to revisit the notion of stewardship of the earth in relation to time and history. Both scripture and African culture affirm that we receive the earth, in its current state, as a gift from the ancestors who have gone before us. This means that we need to recognise with thanks their contribution towards keeping and honouring the creator's creation. However, it also infers that we must learn from their mistakes in order that we should not repeat them within our lifetime. Moreover, there is not only a need to look 'back' upon history, but also to maintain a forward-looking perspective. The earth also belongs to those generations that will come after us. God expects us to hold the land and the resources of our planet in trust for them.

Fourthly, there is a need to correct the false western ideology that the land 'belongs to the people. Instead, we belong to the land.'[32] This point corrects

---

31 'The Earth Belongs to God' http://www.neccsa.org.za/Documents-Earth belongs to God.htm (accessed 22 December 2007 9h34)
32 'The Earth Belongs to God,' http://www.neccsa.org.za/Documents-Earth belongs to God.htm (accessed 22 December 2007 9h38).

the false theology of an anthropocentric cosmic order. Rather, we recognise, as we read in scripture, that the earth and all that is upon it belongs to the Lord. Moreover, we have come from the earth and shall return to it. It also breaks down the false dualism that has been created between persons and creation: 'We are not living on the earth; we are part of the earth's biosphere.'[33]

Finally, we need to recapture the reality that God is at the centre of all creation. People and their needs, as well as the earth and its bountiful resources, all belong to God and find their proper perspective in relation to the God who creates them. As a result of this, the African Christian theologians have called all peoples to respond to our current predicament by:

- Confessing that we have not always treated the earth and its resources as God would have us do.

- Acknowledging that God has given us the responsibility of caring for the earth, and all peoples, by being generous and responsible stewards.

- Committing ourselves to work towards the creation of a sustainable world where no person has too much, and no person has too little. In order to do this we shall have to address economic, political and social structures with courage and grace.

- Calling the leaders of structures of power and authority (including those in the Churches) to prioritise and promote the well-being of the earth and all of God's creatures and creation; and to resist greed and self-interest.

- Praying for the healing of the earth and the peoples of the earth.

CONCLUSION

This paper has presented the sad reality that often socio-economic 'red' concerns have taken prominence over environmental 'green' concerns. This

---

33 'The Earth Belongs to God,' http://www.neccsa.org.za/Documents-Earth belongs to God.htm (accessed 22 December 2007 9h47).

is not only the case in Southern Africa, but is a global trend. At the heart of this problem is a mistaken understanding that 'red' and 'green' concerns are not fundamentally interconnected.

This paper also considered how the favouring of 'red' concerns, at the expense of 'green' concerns, is affecting some of the poorest inhabitants of the world – those who live in the informal settlements of Southern Africa.

In conclusion, some pointers were given, from African traditional religion and African Christian theology, that may help to balance both 'red' and 'green' concerns as the Church strives to develop a theology of sustainable development.

If it is indeed true that 'The earth is the Lord's, and all that is in it ...' (Psalm 24: 1), then it is surely true that we cannot afford to tackle urgent social issues at the expense of apparently less urgent but ultimately more catastrophic environmental issues. I would therefore contend that any Church that chooses to focus exclusively on 'red' rather than 'green' issues is running the risk of seeking short-term popular gains rather than considering long-term sustainability for humanity and the planet that nourishes our life.

True leadership requires the courage to do more than address the concerns of the moment in pursuit of popular approval. In the final analysis, when God evaluates our stewardship of resources, both human and natural, how will we measure up?

BIBLICAL PRINCIPLES AND THEIR ECONOMIC IMPLICATIONS

Alan Storey

It is hard to get riches with justice,
to keep them with equality, and to spend them with love.
Walter Rauschenbusch – Christianity and Social Crisis

ECONOMICS AND THEOLOGY[34]

'Economics is too important to the human enterprise to leave in the hands of economists alone' (Wogaman 1986: 3). This is true for a number of reasons. It is true first because economics affects us all – the poor and the rich, the young and the old, clergy and laity, believers and non-believers. Exactly *how* each of us is affected by any particular economic issue may well vary, but that all of us *are* affected is certain.

Second, it is true because there is no such thing as 'pure economics'. 'We

---

34 This chapter is an edited version of an unpublished research paper submitted in 2006 as a requirement for the M Phil in Applied Ethics at St Augustine College of South Africa. This portion is republished here with kind permission from St Augustine College.

must not only know what we want to achieve, but also what we are *supposed* to want to achieve and for what reasons ... economics is not, and can never be, a 'value free science' (Nürnberger 1998: 6). All economic systems are based upon value judgements – value judgements that stand upon particular understandings of human nature, perhaps even divine nature, and reality itself. These value judgements form the deeper frame of reference for the economic theory and are mostly hidden within the given economic theory. When these hidden values are brought to the surface however, it is clear that economics is itself rooted in many other disciplines, not least theology, and therefore duly requiring their input. Thus the work of Richard Niebuhr helpfully reminds us that 'behind questions of action lie interpretation and identity. Who we understand ourselves to be and how we interpret what is going on will determine what we think we ought to do' (Niebuhr in Spohn 1999: 3). This is of vital importance because, no matter how effective and efficient an economic system may be, if it does not ultimately rest upon a true understanding of humanity and creation and how the Creator has intended things to be, it will soon fail and cause great suffering in the process of its rise and fall.

Third, it is true because ultimately economics touches and shapes the entire world in which we live: 'The Greek word from which we derive economy, *oikonomia*, is a compound of *oikos*, household, and *nomos,* law or management. *Economy* means literally "the law or the management of the household"' (Meeks 1989: 3). In ancient times, the term 'house' or 'household' was freely used to express the various ways in which people shared life together, from families and clans to tribes and nations. In those times economics referred quite simply to the way in which households behaved and were managed, and that impacted upon the wellbeing of everyone in the community as a whole.

This understanding thrusts economics directly into the realm of theology, for the well-being of people is one of God's primary concerns. Indeed, God is not a neutral bystander when it comes to economics, but has some passionate convictions about how people should go about sharing life together. Thus, to think theologically about economics is to allow God's passionate convictions about the right ordering of 'households' (in the broadest sense of that word) to inform our convictions and shape our actions around our common life together.

ECONOMICS AND SCRIPTURE

Scripture does not provide any simple proof texts regarding the form that economic structures should take within societies or organisations. Douglas Meeks correctly states: 'There is ... no scientific economic theory in the modern sense in the Bible, even though the Bible is centrally concerned with economy' (Meeks 1989: 3). However, he continues, 'even if the Bible cannot be immediately translated into economic theory and policy, faith in the God of the Bible has economic implications that derive from who God is and from God's own redemptive history with the world' (Meeks 1989: 4).

Faith in the God of the Bible has economic implications because it shapes our understanding of creation's original purpose and ultimate goal including the original purpose and ultimate goal of humanity. This in turn shapes our values, which then form the deeper frame of reference for economic theory. Ultimately economic theory is called to embody God's passionate convictions about the right ordering of 'households' which honour God's intention for God's creation.

Both Philip Wogaman (1986) and Walter Owensby (1988) make helpful contributions toward the connection between faith in the God of the Bible and consequent economic implications. Drawing mainly upon these scholars, here is a list of ten biblical principles that have certain economic implications:

1. Stewardship

Both Wogaman (1986: 37) and Owensby (1988: xvi) cite the importance of the Biblical principle of stewardship. According to Scripture, human beings are called to be stewards for God. Stewards are people who live to please their Master and not themselves. They also know that they are not the true owner of that over which they have been given responsibility. Stewardship recognises the Biblical truth that everything belongs to God: 'The earth is the Lord's and all that is in it, the world, and those who live in it' (Psalm 24: 1). Therefore all we have is a gift from God and is to be 'subordinated to the purposes of the Creator' (Wogaman 1986: 37). This means that even property rights are not absolute. As stewards we are called to nurture and care for everything in unselfish ways for the benefit of all people everywhere and for all time. Everything is on loan to us to use to fulfil God's intentions. In the words of Pope Paul VI:

> God intended the earth and all it contains for the use of all men [sic] and peoples, so created goods should flow fairly to all, regulated by justice and accompanied by charity. Whatever forms property may take according to legitimate custom and changing circumstances, this universal destiny of the earth's resources should always be borne in mind. In his use of them, man [sic] should regard his legitimate possessions not simply as his own but as common in the sense that they can benefit others as well as himself. But everybody has a right to a share of the earth's goods sufficient for himself and his family (*Gaudium et Spes* 1966: 69).

> At the heart of Biblical faith is the conviction that we are the managers of everything and the owners of nothing. The concept of stewardship builds economic order upon the responsibility of using all of God's resources to benefit all of God's people for all ages. There is no room for narrow maximisation of self, class, nation, or generation. (Owensby 1988: xvii)

2. Human Dignity of All Persons

Like the Sabbath, economics was made for humanity and not humanity for economics. Economics is to serve the aim of promoting and protecting human dignity:

> But the basic purpose of production is not mere increase of goods, nor gain, nor domination, but the service of man [sic] – of man in his entirety, with attention to his material needs and his intellectual, moral and spiritual demands in the prop-

er order; the needs of any man, let us add, any group of men, and race or religion. (*Gaudium et Spes*: 64)

Though the word 'dignity' is not found in Genesis, the concept of human dignity has been strongly developed by its declaration of *Imago Dei. Imago Dei* is the Bible's testimony to the sacred dignity of *all* persons in that at the heart of each person God has etched God's own affirming image: 'So God created humankind in his image, in the image of God he created them; male and female he created them' (Genesis 1: 27). And further, according to Genesis, God looked upon all that God had made, including the human person and recognised 'it was very good' (Genesis 1: 31). On this basis, according to the Judeo-Christian view, all people are endowed with an 'original blessing' (Fox 1983) of intrinsic dignity. Humanity's inviolable dignity is affirmed throughout the Scriptures in the way protection was offered to the widows and orphans (Deuteronomy 24: 3) and in the way God continues to claim us as friends through Jesus, even though 'we were God's enemies' (Romans 5: 10).

According to Catholic Social Teaching:

> To speak of the dignity of the human person is to speak of the worth or value of the concrete existing human being. Those who use the phrase imply that human beings have a value or worth qualitatively different from that of anything else in the world, that this dignity is inalienable in the sense that it can never be lost, and that it is never permissible to merely use a human being to attain some end or purpose (Dwyer 1994: 724).

The reason human dignity can never be lost is that it is 'unearned, un-manufactured, and unmaintained. Like an involuntary bodily function such as the heartbeat, it simply occurs naturally, by design, without any thought or effort being devoted to it by the individual who possesses it' (Stetson 1998: 15). This differs from extrinsic dignity that is 'fundamentally behavioural ... and conditional on the fulfilment of certain rules, norms, or expectations' (Stetson 1998: 17). But 'while human dignity is not directly dependent upon material considerations, it is nevertheless the case that the growth and development of our social and moral capacities require that our physical needs be met' (SACBC 1999: 24).

This unconditional nature of humanity's intrinsic dignity thus forbids all forms of discrimination whether national, religious, racial, sexual or economic. No one should then claim that God has ordained some people to be poor and others to be rich. The Bible testifies to a God who 'shows no partiality' (Acts 10: 34) between people or nations, and nor should our economic policies. Nor should poverty be viewed as part of God's original design of reality and even less as a necessary incentive for a successful economic policy. 'Respect for human dignity demands that workers be treated as more than just another 'input' along with capital, machinery and technology' (SACBC 1999: 24).

3. The Priority of Grace over Works

Wogaman (1986: 34) draws our attention to the priority of Grace as God's way of relating to the world: 'Grace is the undeserved love of God to all' (MCSA Minutes 1952: 216–224) By grace, God does not treat us as we *deserve* to be treated, but rather as we *need* to be treated. God does so to set us free to enjoy life in all its fullness. 'For by grace you have been saved through faith, and this is not your own doing; it is the gift of God – not the result of works, so that no one may boast' (Ephesians 2: 8–9). And 'God makes his sun rise on the evil and on the good, and sends rain on the righteous and on the unrighteous' (Matthew 5: 45).

Grace is God's initiating love actively seeking to reconcile all of creation to God's self. John Wesley spoke of this as 'prevenient grace' that 'comes before our need and our request' (Lewis 1954, 1962: 66). Contrary to popular belief, God does not only help those who can help themselves, but rather, by grace, God helps those who *cannot* help themselves.

Grace silences the proud cry that 'I am a self-made person' as well as the boast that 'I have made my wealth through hard work alone'. Grace reminds us that there are always factors other than our own efforts that have played important roles in determining levels of economic reward. Grace testifies to the truth that sometimes we get given far more than we deserve.

Besides, the notion that people are to get what they deserve is illusionary in practice because 'we never really *know* who earns or deserves everything. In the way the world actually works, luck and deception play important roles. Rewards as well as penalties are often grossly disproportionate to accomplishments or failures' (Wogaman 1986: 75).

Then to be fair, the bottom-line of every economy should be grace. Here grace would be expressed as the provision of a certain level of economic security for all. This would go a long way to protect the marginalised poor from falling outside of the formal economy:

> if justice is patterned in accordance with the priority of grace, then economic goods should be produced and distributed in such a way as to enhance human well-being and self-acceptance and communal fellow feeling without asking first whether people have deserved what they receive. (Wogaman 1986: 35)

Social security systems like Child Support Grants and the proposal of a Basic-Income-Grant[35] (BIG) are examples of an economy patterned by grace.

4. Vocation

Wogaman (1986: 36) creatively balances the priority of Grace with the importance of vocation. This is an important corollary to the previous principle. God calls us to work. The Bible speaks of humanity as God's 'holy partners in a heavenly calling' (Hebrews 3: 1). 'We do not have to earn or deserve God's grace in order to have it given to us; but God's grace remains unfulfilled in our lives without active response on our part' (Wogaman 1986: 36). We are saved by grace 'for good works' (Ephesians 2: 10). As we have emphasised God's gift of grace, so now we point to the high standards of discipleship to which all of us have been called. All people are therefore called to respond to the gift of God's grace with gratitude and generosity expressed in the service of the betterment of all and of creation as a whole:

---

35   The advocates of BIG suggest that providing a universal amount of R100 per month will eliminate some of the social problems people face. See Chagunda in Praxis 2/3: 2003.

'Thieves must stop stealing; rather let them labour and work honestly with their own hands, so as to have something to share with the needy' (Ephesians 4: 28). This means we are called to work not only to earn a *living* but to earn a *giving*. It is our vocation to assist God in meeting the world's deep needs. Describing the nature of vocation, Frederick Buechner (1993: 119) writes: 'The place God calls you to is the place where your deep gladness and the world's deep hunger meet'.

In the Bible vocation is not limited to individuals. The Bible testifies to the vocational call of the Hebrew nation to be 'a covenant people and a light for the Gentiles' (Isaiah 42: 6b). Institutions and organisations like the church and business all have a vocation to be fulfilled, as Walter Wink motivates:

> The church is commanded to preach about God's 'manifold wisdom' to the principalities and powers, calling them back to their divine vocation, which is to serve the general welfare. God does not call corporations to make a profit. God calls them, rather, to make and keep human life more human. Profit is not the end, but the means; it is the reward corporations receive for serving the public good. (Wink 1996: 9)

5. Community

Wogaman (1986: 35) highlights the importance of social relationships, as does Owensby (1988: xvii): 'Economics must be concerned about two things at once: the physical needs of people and the effect of economic organisation on relationships' (Wogaman 1986: 35). God is as concerned with how much each person has to eat as God is concerned with how authentically life-giving our relationships are with each other around the table. Even if the poorest of the poor have their most basic needs met, if they are so much poorer than others it will be nearly impossible for them 'to relate as brother and sister to the very affluent' (Wogaman 1986: 35). In other words, a person's well-being should be measured in relational terms and never simply reduced to material categories. High levels of inequality break down community. Jesus is most concerned that we live into the truth of our 'oneness' with all people (John 17), recognising that there is only one family to which we belong and that is the human family. The Bible's emphasis is on community and not individuals:

> The 'individual' is an abstraction that can fit into the thought pattern of modern economics. A critical doctrine of God, however, should show that God is not a radical individual but rather a community of diverse persons that finds unity in self-giving love rather than in substantialist or subjectivist principles of identity ... the persons of the Trinity is a model of interrelationships of the members of the household that God intends. All the persons of the triune community have their own characteristics and their own tasks. Yet they are constituted as persons precisely by their relationships with the other persons of the community ... the same should be said for human economic community. There is in reality no such thing as a radically individual and isolated human being. We are what we are as a result of being constituted by our relationships with the other members of the communities in which we live. (Meeks 1989: 11–12)

This raises questions about the right to maximise personal profits. 'The goal of an economic system, therefore, is not to guarantee the right of the individual to acquire and accumulate all that personal ability and drive make possible. The goal is to provide for the needs of the global human community in a way that will draw people and nations together rather than further divide them' (Owensby 1988: xvii–xviii). This means that we have a responsibility not only for our own generation but also future generations. As the *NGO Forum Treaty on Alternative Economic Models* from Rio de Janeiro explains: 'Economic life must also be organised in such a way that it enhances rather than destroys the environment and safeguards natural resources for the use of future generations' (Duchrow 1995: 143–144).

The Bible strongly opposes an isolated viewpoint which suggests that 'we in the rich world are not rich because poor people in the poor world are poor, nor vice versa – they are not poor because we are rich' (John Kay in Foster and Newell, ed. 2005: 48). The Bible says we are all linked in very interdependent ways. 'If one part suffers, every part suffers with it' (1 Corinthians 12: 26). Therefore, the way each of us lives our lives impacts on everyone else both now and into the future.

Not only the Bible speaks of our universal unity, but science also speaks of the interconnected nature of the cosmos: 'We know from the quantum insights of post-modern science that everything in creation interconnects. The totality of the created order is a kind of hidden but immensely real network of interrelation' (Sims 1997: 29).

6. Justice

God is a 'lover of justice' says the Psalmist (Psalm 99: 4). According to Walter Brueggemann justice is what God values most. A popular understanding of justice often equates justice with 'bringing criminals to the punishment they deserve.' This is *not* how the Bible thinks about justice. Rather, according to the Bible: 'Justice is to sort out what belongs to whom, and to return it to them ... Justice concerns precisely a right reading of social reality, of social power and of social goods ... the agenda is consistently economic. The real issues concerning justice have to do with access and control of life-goods' (Brueggemann 1986: 5–8). It is this understanding of justice with which God's heart resonates because it is justice that when practised protects the vulnerable of society. The Market propagates the survival of the fittest, but the Bible speaks of the survival of the feeblest.

It is the community's responsibility to secure fairness for all with special attention given to the weakest and most vulnerable of society (Owensby 1988: xviii). A community is only as strong as the weakest within it. The repeated imperative to care for the widows, orphans and foreigners is the Bible's way of reminding society to care for the marginalised. God is most concerned how the vulnerable poor of the world are treated.

Dom Helder Camara's statement 'when justice is the issue, charity is a sin' remains true. The Bible says that God not only hears the cries of the poor but will act on their behalf for their liberation. God longs for the poor to have good news (Luke 4: 18). This does not mean the poor are any less sinful than the rich, but what it does mean is that the poor are most sinned against and God will not tolerate it: 'Woe to him who builds his house by unrighteousness, and his upper rooms by injustice; who makes his neighbours work for nothing, and does not give them their wages' (Jeremiah 22: 13). The repeated call of the scriptures is for there to be a 'fair balance' (NRSV) or 'equality' (NIV) reflected, for example, in 2 Corinthians 8: 13–15. 'It is ultimately no privilege to be rich where others are poor; it is a burden' (Wogaman 1986: 76).

A 'fair balance' or 'equality' does not mean 'sameness'. As Douglas Meeks explains:

> Equality means the thrust to abolish the differences that result from wealth, racial and sexual supremacy, ecological rape, and meritocratic privilege. Equality works against the experience of subordination. It works against some people having to fawn, defer, bow, and scrape because other people or groups have power over them. The equalitarian impetus of God's economy is against all forms of domination by which the powerful 'grind the faces of the poor'. It intends the end of the master-slave relationship. The egalitarian thrust of God's economy is meant to serve freedom. It does not aim at eliminating differences among human beings ... Rather, equality in the household of God means that radically different persons embrace and yet remain different. We do not have to be the same or have the same amount of things. What God's household [economy] seeks to eliminate, is domination over others, which prevents their access to what they need in order to keep their calling to be God's image, child, disciple, and friend. (Meeks 1989: 11)

Jesus, like Mary before him, spoke of the great reversal of the ways of domination – where the last will be first and the lowly will be lifted up. Above all the poor are the real blessed ones (Luke 6: 20), not because they are morally superior to the rich, but because they carry within them the hunger and thirst for the management of the world household to change, unlike the rich who are content with the status quo. The poor are blessed in that they embody the anguished frustration of God for the way things are in the world as well as embody the dream of God for the way things should, and ultimately will, be in the end.

7. Abundance and Abundant Life

Another passionate conviction of the God of the Bible is that abundance, rather than scarcity, is the true nature of the world:

> The Gospels portray Jesus as the one who brings the overwhelm-
> ing grace of God into the intimate companionship of human life.
> His person and work, his word and deed, the questions he asks
> and the challenge he presents, the commands he makes and the
> pleas he answers, the stories he tells and the sacrifice he makes
> – all are too much for the people he meets. And the abundance
> of God lays bare the scarcity of sin (Wells 2006: 23).

According to the testimony of the Bible there is more than enough for eve-ryone's needs (note: *needs* not *wants*) to be abundantly satisfied. This is true from the Manna-filled wilderness story (Exodus 16) to Jesus feeding the five thousand (Mark 6: 30–44), all of which seek to 'reveal the reality of abundance beneath the illusion of scarcity' (Palmer 1990: 137). Therefore poverty in any form should never be tolerated. Poverty in every form goes against the very purpose of Jesus who 'came that they may have life, and have it abundantly' (John 10: 10).

An economic model based on scarcity provokes fear – fear that there will not be enough – fear that *I* will not have enough. This fear moves a person to hoard. Hoarding leads to competition – and competition to conflict and finally, conflict to war – with the end result of the breakdown of human family and community: 'Tragically, every time we act on the scarcity as-sumption, we help create a world in which scarcity becomes a cruel reality' (Palmer 1990: 125).

Acting upon the Biblical principle of abundance leads to the opposite of fear, namely, to love. Love leads to sharing – and sharing to co-operation and finally to compassionate community. The abundance assumption always trusts that when a little is shared it becomes a lot, while at the same time knowing that a little only becomes a lot *once* it has been shared. The economic implications of abundance are that distribution should be based upon human need and not merely human want. The aim of all economics should be abundant life for all.[36]

8. Generosity

The most famous verse in the Bible speaks about generosity: 'For God so loved the world, that God gave' (John 3: 16). Generosity is part of God's nature. As people born in God's image (Genesis 1: 27) generosity is part of humanity's nature too. We have been created by God to be generous. We are born to give and to give sacrificially as God has given generously and sacrificially toward us. This means that the life that God intends for us cannot be fully known unless we live generously.

'The great moral question of our time is how to move from greed to generosity' (Foster 1985, 1987: 86). Economic policy should therefore encourage and enable sacrifice as opposed to selfishness. Sharing, as opposed to having, should be the number one virtue that economics underwrites.

It is through generosity that we express our gratitude towards God's gift of grace and it is by generosity that we partner God in meeting the needs of this broken world. As Archbishop Rowan Williams says: 'All gifts are given so as to be given again' (Foster and Newell 2005: 69).

Living generously also opens us to abundance. 'Give generously to him and do so without a grudging heart; then because of this the Lord your God will bless you in all your work and in everything you put your hand to' (Deuteronomy 15: 10). Being careful to distance ourselves from the heresy

---

36   For a detailed presentation and critique of life-giving economic alternatives see Ulrich Duchrow (1995) as well as the 2002 Kairos Europa publication entitled, *Economy in the Service of Life – Churches in the Ecumenical Process for Globalising Justice.* www.kairoseuropa.de

of prosperity teaching, it must be stated that we are not generous in order to receive. That is not our motivation. Yet it is equally true that when we are generous, we always receive. In some strange but wonderful way, that which we give away determines what we will have most abundantly. One of the gifts given to the generous is freedom. Generosity secures freedom in that it liberates us from the choking effects of greed and fear. Giving generously is what subverts the corrosive power of wealth in one's life.

9. Freedom

God not only longs for our freedom, but tirelessly works to enable it. In the preamble to the *Decalogue,* God's gift of freedom is announced: 'I am the Lord your God, who brought you out of the land of Egypt, out of the house of bondage' (Exodus 20: 2). Years later St Paul implores the Christians in Galatia to remember that: 'For freedom Christ has set us free' (Galatians 5: 1). Humanity is born to be free. 'The human soul is made for freedom … Systems that violate such freedom are doomed to topple in the revolt of subjugated children, oppressed employees, and tyrannized citizens, however long it takes' (Sims 1997: 10 and 29). We have witnessed the truth of this in South Africa's recent history.

God has given humanity the gift of freedom to live life this way or that, the freedom to love or to fear, the freedom to be generous or greedy, the freedom to be merciful or hate-filled, the freedom to seek truthfulness or deception. Human persons are not pre-programmed robots or wind-up toys with a path pre-determined from on high. God has given humanity freedom because God desires to be in a loving relationship with people, not a controlling relationship with mindless puppets. Without freedom a love relationship is not possible because in order for there to be love, there must first of all be freedom. 'Freedom is the air that love breathes – without it love suffocates and dies' (Storey 2002: 10).

The gift of freedom is however as risky as it is necessary. God's loving gift of freedom is what makes it possible for humanity to enter into a loving relationship with God. Paradoxically, it is also that which enables humanity to reject God and God's household rules. The freedom to be faithful goes hand-in-hand with the freedom to be unfaithful. Despite humanity's freedom to fail, God still takes the risk, always hoping and willing humanity to 'choose life' (Deuteronomy 30: 19), but never removing our freedom to choose death. All economic policy should then strive to protect and serve the freedom of all the people involved.

The principle of freedom also has deep philosophical roots, perhaps most especially in Immanuel Kant who rescued human freedom from the determinism of the world of science in his day. This determinism held that the human person was merely a pre-determined cog in a mechanistic universe. Kant placed human freedom within the rational will of rational agents and therefore outside of science's deterministic reach. It is within the human person's true self of pure intelligence that Kant held onto the human person's capacity for free self-determination, which was beyond empirical examination. Kant's safeguard of human freedom is seen most notably in his categorical imperative to 'act so that you treat humanity, whether in your own person or in that of another, as an end and never as a means only' (Beck 1959: 31).

Kant's categorical imperative is perhaps the closest non-religious reformulation of the Golden Rule of Jesus to 'love your neighbour as yourself' (Mark 12: 31): 'Free human beings are those who are free from themselves, and not for themselves but for others' (Sobrino 1988: 61). True freedom is the fruit of love and is realised through faithfulness to God. God's gift of freedom is a freedom endowed with the responsibility to show self-control and collective restraint. It is not the freedom of unrestrained profit taking. God's love of justice 'sets limits for both poverty and wealth' (Waskow 1997: 34). Individual consumption should never override communal compassion. 'Enough is enough, and there are limits to what you may expect or demand; limits set by consideration for the other and by a recognition of your own place in the whole scheme of things' (Taylor 1975: 60).

Furthermore, God's gift of freedom is not limited to the human person but rather impregnates the entire cosmos. This means that society as a whole, and economic structures in particular, is not fixed firm forever. They are 'neither determined by a natural principle nor closed according to a universally defined human nature ... in principle everything about economy can be rethought and changed' (Meeks 1989: 9–10). We sometimes tend to speak of the 'market' as if it is a fixed natural entity. To do so is to deny that the market is people – free people who have designed and established exist-ing economic policy in a particular way and which free people can redesign and transform into new and even radically different economic policy.

10. Original Sin

Wogaman (1986: 37) reminds us that we dare not naively ignore the sad truth of 'original sin' within the human condition: 'Original sin is the doc-trine about the impact of the first sin ever committed on the spiritual state of every human being from the first moment of his or her existence' (Gay-bba 2004: 151). Both Catholics and Protestants 'agreed on the effects that this had on the individual, namely: 1) being born lacking the transforming presence of God in one's life; 2) being born at the mercy of one's selfish desires; 3) being born therefore with a nature that leads one to sin' (Gaybba 2004: 152).

In this it is acknowledged that human persons have a history from the very beginning of taking our God given gift of freedom and using it to declare selfish independence from God. Freedom has been misunderstood to mean, 'anything goes' or 'doing as one pleases'. Instead of using our freedom to freely serve God and love our neighbour, humanity employs it selfishly for self-gain. The human condition is corrupted towards a com-fortable self-centeredness. It is the Biblical assertion that we have 'fallen' from God's original and glorious intentions and that we need help to do the right thing: 'I can will what is right, but I cannot do it. For I do not do the good I want, but the evil I do not want is what I do' (Romans 7: 18b–19).

'This tendency towards self-centeredness has important implications for economics. It suggests that no economic system predicated entirely on hu-man goodness is likely to be successful and that economics ... needs to insti-tutionalise protections against the destructive possibilities of self-centred behaviour' (Wogaman 1986: 38). Economic policy should attempt to both bring out the best in people and protect against the worst in people.

The Year of Jubilee[37] (Leviticus 25) was one such protection mechanism that the Hebrew people practised in order to 'make forever impossible the permanent concentration of productive power and wealth in the hands of some elite group, resulting in the impoverishment of the many' (Owensby 1988: xvii).

Although some theologians doubt whether Jubilee legislation was ever practised in Biblical Israel, the Year of Jubilee was the honest acknowledgment of the people's self-centred corruption by recognising that over time (fifty years), the community would more than likely be divided into haves and have-nots. Since this is unacceptable to God, it should therefore be corrected through the redistribution of land and resources, enabling everyone – rich and poor – to start over.

'Sin is always present in human economy, no matter what the economy's structure. But sin cannot be made a justification of an economic system. Sin is no excuse for capitalism or socialism, nor can either claim to be a solution to sin' (Meeks 1989: 10). It is important to state that, although economics should seek to safeguard us against our fallen nature, the vision of economic policy should not be determined by it, and humanity's fallen nature should certainly never be relied upon to grease the wheels of an economic system. In accordance with Biblical principles, self-sacrifice (or generosity), and not self-centeredness, should be the celebrated virtue of any given economic policy.

This list of ten Biblical principles is by no means a complete list, but it serves to make the point that faith in the God of the Bible does indeed have economic implications.

Within the Bible itself we witness how the Hebrew people allowed the principles of God's passionate convictions to guide their household management. Their witness should serve as our guide.

PRINCIPLE, PERSONAL, POLICY, PRACTICE AND POLITICS

For example it is stated, 'There will, however, be no one in need among you' (Deuteronomy 15: 4). The people would not only personalise this principle

---

37   See Kraybill (1978, 1990: 89–107) and Harris (1996).

but they would establish an economic policy to honour it in their daily management of their shared life together. So we read, 'When you reap the harvest of your land, you shall not reap to the very edges of your field, or gather the gleanings of your harvest. You shall not strip your vineyard bare, or gather the fallen grapes of your vineyard; you shall leave them for the poor and the alien: I am the Lord your God.' (Leviticus 19: 9–10). This policy honours the principle that no one should be in need, by enabling all people to be free to feed off the leftover produce of others.

This also honours the principles we have mentioned above: stewardship, human dignity, grace, justice, community, abundance and generosity. Now perhaps after some practice of this policy some people were deciding not to work but rather to harvest the work of others. In other words they were no longer simply gathering grapes or grain to feed themselves, they were now gathering grapes and grain to sell at the market place. To make money off the work of others was deemed unfair. It also denied the principle of vocation, not to mention giving stark evidence for the corrupted self-centeredness of human nature. So to protect against this we read, 'If you go into your neighbour's vineyard, you may eat your fill of grapes, as many as you wish, but you shall not put any in a container. If you go into your neighbour's standing grain, you may pluck the ears with your hand, but you shall not put a sickle to your neighbour's standing grain.' (Deuteronomy 23: 24–25).

In this example it is important to note that the Hebrew people's faith journey that began with the principles of God's passionate convictions was not reduced to a private or personal morality. It was fleshed out into economic policy, tested with daily practice and refined with more economic policy that ultimately shaped the politics or the human community of their day. In this single example we see that all ten of the Biblical principles mentioned above have been taken into consideration.

With regard to our economic choices we too should allow God's passionate convictions to shape our values and form the deeper frame of reference. In this way we do not start by asking questions about what we should do, but rather we ask questions concerning the true identity of God and humanity within all of creation. This list of Biblical principles will help us with these important questions of identity. In this way our economic choices will be a more faithful sign of God's original purpose and ultimate goal revealed to us by Jesus of Nazareth.

MISUSED PARABLES

But what about those passages of scripture that seemingly state alternative or even contradictory principles that in turn validate different values to the ten mentioned above? Am I simply choosing the principles that I like, according to a pre-judged set of personal values, while ignoring all those that I do not like? Of course there is always a danger of this and a humble openness to be corrected is always wise. It may then be helpful to reflect upon two further passages of scripture to help build my case. These two passages of scripture are parables of Jesus and I believe that their meaning has been repeatedly misused to ironically propagate the very opposite message to that which Jesus originally intended.

The first passage of scripture is one of the most frequently used by people looking to find scriptural backing for an economic policy that is rooted in opposing values to the ten already mentioned above. It is interesting to note that the scripture I am about to refer to was the most quoted in a survey I conducted to discover whether stipend equity was feasible amongst all clergy in the MCSA. In every case people were quoting it with the intention of legitimising the large pay differentials that exist between clergy. When this passage of scripture is viewed within its correct context, however, we may be shocked to discover its true meaning and how people throughout the ages (including those who filled out my survey) have not only misunderstood the scripture, but have misused it to support economic policy and practice that contradicts God's passionate convictions about the management of the world's household.

WHEN THE MASTER IS *NOT* GOD

The passage of scripture I am referring to is known to us as the parable of the talents, found in Matthew 25: 14–30 (also in Luke 19: 11–27). It seems that for many people this parable provides divine approval for the maximi-sation of individual profits. On the surface this certainly seems to be the case. However, it may be helpful if we ask a few questions about the text: Why is this parable not introduced with Jesus' familiar phrase: 'The King-dom of Heaven is like ...'? What is the significance of the fact that a single 'talent' was equal to fifteen years wages? How does this parable challenge our understanding of God revealed to us in Jesus? To answer these and other questions I rely upon the work of Ched Myers (2001) and William Herzog II (1994).

A popular reading of this parable of the talents makes for a very disturbing story indeed. It replaces God's covenantal relationship with humanity with a contractual relationship that once broken is not redeemed but cast aside.

> It seems to promote ruthless business practices (v.20), usury (v.27), and the cynical view that the rich will only get richer, while the poor become destitute (v.29). Moreover, if we assume, as does the traditional reading, that the master is a figure for God, it is a severe portrait indeed: an absentee lord (v.15) who cares only about profit maximisation (v.21) this character is hard-hearted (v.24) and ruthless (v.30) ... (Myers 2001: 41).

In order to soften the harshness of the parable, many interpretations have denied its economic nature by seeing the 'talents' as something other than sums of money.

Despite these concerns articulated by Myers, this parable has consist-ently been interpreted as a parable of the Kingdom of Heaven, where the master is seen to represent God and as such it has often been used as a scriptural validation for wage inequality. Myers goes on to ask whether we have not 'imposed upon the parable our capitalist presumptions about the glories of a system that rewards 'venture capital' and thus read the story exactly backwards' (Myers 2001: 41).

According to Myers, Jesus employed 'two basic kinds of parables: those that attempted to unmask and critique the way the world *really was* ... and those that offered a vision of the way the world *could* be' (Myers 2001: 40). In this light it is important to note that Jesus does not introduce this parable of the talents with the familiar words: 'The Kingdom of Heaven is like'. It seems that many readers have failed to notice this, and have simply presumed that all of Jesus' parables were about the Kingdom of Heaven. The parables that do not have the 'kingdom-of-heaven-is-like' introduction make more sense when read as parables that critique the way the world *really was*. These parables expose the injustices of Jesus' own social, economic, political and religious context, and should not be read as metaphorical examples of Kingdom life:

> The first two slaves double their master's investment (25: 16–17). Though lauded by modern interpreters, this feat would have elicited disgust from the first-century audience ... Anthropology has shown that in traditional Mediterranean society, the ideal was stability, not self-advancement. Anyone trying to accumulate inordinate wealth imperilled the equilibrium of society and was thus understood to be dishonourable. (Myers 2001: 42)

Therefore, the so-called 'good stewards' would fall into this dishonourable category. This makes more sense when we remember that a 'talent' was worth around fifteen years wages. Five talents is then equivalent to seventy-five years wages. This is an incredibly large sum of money.

The third slave is next up to give an account. And Myers suggests that the slave who buried (or planted) the master's talent may have been involved with some prophetic humour:

> considering that many of Jesus' audience were farmers, there may be some wry peasant humour here. Those who work the land know that all true wealth comes from God, the source of rain, sunshine, seed and soil. But this silver talent, when 'sown', produced no fruit! Here is the clash between two economic worldviews: the traditional agrarian notion of 'use-value' and the elite's currency-based system of 'exchange-value.' Money cannot grow the natural way like seed, only unnaturally, through usury and swindling. Is this symbolic act of

'planting' the talent a case of prophetic tricksterism to reveal that money is not fertile? (Myers 2001: 44)

The third slave challenges those in positions of privilege and power as well as the economic system that benefits them: 'I knew you were a harsh man – you reap where you did not sow, and gather where you did not scatter' (25: 24). With these words, Jesus exposes the truth of injustice that existed in the economic system of his own day. This third slave was a 'whistle blower' for the truth (Herzog II 1994: 150): 'Having unmasked the fact that the master's wealth is entirely derived from the toil of others ... [and] unwilling to participate in this exploitation, this third slave took the money out of circulation where it could no longer be used to dispossess another family farmer' (Myers 2001: 44).

This third slave, considered wicked, wasteful and worthless by the economic system represented by the master (and by so many present-day readers who see the slave as lazy), then suffers a prophet's doom by being cast out into a hell (to be cast out of the dominant economic system on earth) that is for those who don't play by the rules of an economic system that honours self-advancement over social stability and community well-being.

More could be said about this parable of the talents, but the hope is that enough has been said to at least raise serious questions about using this passage of scripture (or others like it) to legitimise economic policy that goes against the ten Biblical principles already stated.

WHEN THE MASTER *IS* GOD

The second passage of Scripture (another parable of Jesus) is also misunderstood and misused, but in quite the opposite way from the first. This parable, which should be taken as a vision of the way the world *could be* according to God's passionate convictions about the management of the world's household, with real day-to-day economic implications attached to it, is avoided by an overly-spiritualised (in the worst sense of the word) meaning given to it. The parable I am referring to is the parable of the labourers in the vineyard found in Matthew 20: 1–16.

Unlike the parable in Matthew 25: 14–30, Jesus introduces this parable as a Kingdom-like story (v.1). It is a story of how God longs for the world to be. In this story we find God as one of the characters, namely the landowner.

This is also a disturbing parable however, especially when we discover that the manager, on the landowner's instructions, pays all the labourers the same wage even though some have toiled all day, while others have only worked an hour or so. No wonder we read that those who had worked all day 'grumbled against the landowner, saying "These last worked only one hour, and you have made them equal to us who have borne the burden of the day and the scorching heat"' (v.11–12).

It seems that in order to make this parable easier to swallow, there has been a strong tendency to 'spiritualise' its meaning. In this 'spiritualised' light, the parable is seen to be referring to the same reward everyone receives when they accept Jesus as Lord of their life. This means that regardless of whether a person's acceptance of Jesus happens early in life or not, even whether it happens during a person's dying breaths; all receive the same heavenly reward in the end. This interpretation may well speak the truth about the saving grace of God, but it denies the real economic nature and challenges of this particular parable, and incorrectly suggests that the parable's meaning is pointing to the heavens above rather than to the earth below.

Could Jesus not be suggesting that managers who operate under God's Kingdom instructions, pay people according to a different principle from that of the profit-driven merit-earned market-world? Could Jesus be saying to us through this parable that 'labour and income in fact are not permitted to become dependent on each other'? (Haan 1991: 64). I think he is. In other words, Kingdom managers pay people not simply according to what they deserve, as a result of the amount of work they have done, but rather according to what they need in order to live. Here we see grace outworking works.

This is an assault on our understanding of fairness! It is also an assault on our wisdom, as it begs the question: 'Who would want to work a full day in the future if they knew they would get paid the same for only working an hour?' The answer: the people who have discovered the joy of their vocation to partner God in the work of reconciling and restoring this broken world.

The sadness of the parable is that those who worked all day find it impossible to join in the celebration of the other labourers who earned the same as a result of the extravagant generosity of the landowner (God figure). The landowner freely sacrifices some profits for the sake of providing a living wage for all the labourers. Here the landowner lives out the Biblical truth that there is an abundance to meet everyone's need.

These two parables challenge the values that legitimise all economies.

GOD'S HOUSEHOLD

In this chapter I have tried to show that it is quite impossible for economics to remain outside the realm of theology. First, because economics affects all people and God is concerned for all people. Second, because if we scratch beneath the surface of economic policy we find the values about the nature of reality that underpin the policy, and theology has not a few things to say about the nature of reality. Third, because the economy is ultimately about the management of the world-household, the world that God so loves.

We have indicated that God is no neutral bystander when it comes to economics, but has passionate convictions about how people should go about sharing life together. The Church is called to give expression to these passionate convictions not only in its prayers and preaching but its practice. The Church is called to live God's household rules into being.

> The Church is God's attempt to build a household that will join God in making the world into home. Theology finds its bearings by asking what kind of household God is trying to build for the sake of God's threatened creation. God's economic work and the economic work to which God calls the disciples of Jesus Christ is different from the economies that human beings normally dream and produce (Meeks 1989: 44).

If God is not a neutral bystander when it comes to economics, then neither should the Church be a neutral bystander. The above-mentioned biblical principles could serve as a guide for the Church to helpfully contribute towards the life-giving management of God's household – the world.

BIBLIOGRAPHY

Beck, L W 1959. *Foundations of the Metaphysics of Morals.* Indianapolis: Macmillan.

Brueggemann, W 1978. *The Prophetic Imagination.* Philadelphia: Fortress Press.

Brueggemann, W 1986. *To Act Justly, Love Tenderly, Walk Humbly: An Agenda for Ministers.* New York: Paulist Press.

Buechner, F 1993, 1973. *Wishful Thinking: A Seeker's ABC.* New York: Harper Collins.

Catholic Bishops' Conference of England and Wales 1996. *The Common Good and the Catholic Church's Social Teaching.* London: Catholic Bishops of England and Wales.

Cook, K S. and Hegtvedt, K A 1983. *Distributive Justice, Equity, and Equality.* Annual Reviews Inc.

Duchrow, U 1995. *Alternatives to Global Capitalism: Drawn from Biblical History, Designed for Political Action.* Germany: International Books with Kairos Europa.

Dwyer, J A (ed) 1994. *The New Dictionary of Catholic Social Thought.* Collegeville, MN: The Liturgical Press.

Foster, C and Newell, E. (eds) 2005. *The Worlds We Live In. Dialogues with Rowan Williams on Global Economics and Politics.* London: Darton, Longman and Todd.

Foster, R 1981. *Freedom of Simplicity.* New York: Harper and Row.

Foster, R 1985, 1987. *Money Sex and Power: The Spiritual Disciplines of Poverty Chastity and Obedience.* London: Hodder and Stoughton.

Fox, M 1983. *Original Blessing. A Primer in Creation Spirituality.* Santa Fe, NM: Bear and Company.

Gaybba, B 2004. *God is a Community. A General Survey of Christian Theology.* Pretoria: UNISA Press.

Haan, R 1991. *The Economics of Honour. Biblical reflections on money and property.* Geneva: WCC.

Haughey, J 1997. *Virtue and Affluence: The Challenge of Wealth.* New York: Sheed and Ward.

Herzog II, W R 1994. *Parables as Subversive Speech: Jesus as Pedagogue of the Oppressed.* Atlanta: John Knox Press.

Kraybill, D B 1978, 1990. *The Upside-down Kingdom.* Scottsdale, Pennsylvania: Herald Press.

Lewis, G P (ed) 1954, 1962. *An Approach to Christian Doctrine*. Cape Town: Methodist Publishing House.

Meeks, M D 1989. *God the Economist – The Doctrine of God and Political Economy*. Philadelphia: Fortress Press.

Methodist Church of Southern Africa 1952. *Minutes of Conference*. Cape Town: Methodist Publishing House.

Myers, C 2001. *The Biblical Vision of Sabbath Economics*. New York: Tell the Word Publishing.

Nurnberger, K 1998. *Beyond Marx and Market: Outcomes of a century of economic experimentation*. Pietermaritzburg: Cluster Publication.

Owensby, W L 1988. *Economics For Prophets. A primer on concepts, realities, and values in our economic system*. Grand Rapids: Eerdmans.

Pope Paul VI 1966. *Gaudium et Spes*. London: Catholic Truth Society.

Rauschenbusch, W 1964, 1991. *Christianity and Social Crisis*. Atlanta: John Knox Press.

Sims, B J 1997. *Servanthood: Leadership for the Third Millennium*. Cambrdge, MA: Cowley Publications.

Sobrino, J 1988. *Spirituality of Liberation: Toward Political Holiness*. Maryknoll, NY: Orbis Books.

Southern African Catholic Bishop's Conference 1999. *Economic Justice in South Africa – A Pastoral Statement*. Pretoria: SACBC Publishing.

Storey, Alan 2002. *Foundations For Discipleship: A Christ Healed Africa for the Healing of the Nations*. Unpublished Manuscript.

Storey, P 2004. *And are we yet Alive? Revisioning our Wesleyan Heritage in the New South Africa*. Cape Town: Methodist Publishing House.

Waskow, A 1997. *Holy Economics: A Rhythm of Worthy Work and Reflective Rest*. Washington DC: Sojourners Magazine. September – October Edition.

Wells, S 2006. *God's Companions. Reimagining Christian Ethics*. Oxford: Blackwell Publishing.

Wink, W 1992. *Engaging the Powers: Discernment and Resistance in a World of Domination*. Philadelphia: Fortress Press.

Wink, W 1996. The Gospel and Work, in *The Living Pulpit, Work*. July/September. Vol. 5. No. 3. New York: Living Pulpit. Inc.

Wink, W 1998. *The Powers That Be: Theology for a New Millennium*. Philadelphia: Fortress Press.

Wogaman, J P 1986. *Economics and Ethics: A Christian Inquiry*. Philadelphia: Fortress Press.

READING THE FAITH THROUGH WOMEN'S EYES

Reading the Bible from a different perspective

Madika Sibeko

The Methodist Church, of which the majority of members are women, was one of the first mainline Churches to ordain women. One would expect this Church, therefore, through its Education Unit, to expose all ministers in training to the skills of reading the biblical text from the perspectives of the marginalised. In this paper I reflect on the work of students from John Wesley College (JWC) in Pretoria. Their views on the challenges of the TEEC (Theological Education by Extension College) course 'Reading the faith through women's eyes' are discussed, as are their fears concerning bringing about changes in Societies and Circuits back home as a consequence of doing this course. This paper not only attempts to show how the Bible has been used traditionally to serve patriarchal agendas in our Churches, with the consequent marginalisation of women, but also how the Bible can be used to empower and bring about changes in the lives of those who make up the majority in the Church.

INTRODUCTION

This chapter has been motivated by my involvement with seminary students at JWC during 2007 and their contributions in class during the 'Reading the Bible through Women's Eyes' course (7/6378).

One of the topics with which the students grappled concerned the problem of God's gender. For instance, most male and a few female students argued for the maleness of God. In our discussions, I recall these students finding it difficult to accept that God is beyond gender and that their use of words like 'He' and 'Father' in relation to God was problematic for those who had experienced abuse from their own father figures.

On the other hand, ideas of the femaleness of God would be equally problematic for those who had experienced abuse from their mother figures or, for that matter, those who had been abandoned as children. However, when the paradigm shift in their thinking took place, and they all understood the problems created by the traditional male images of God, the class determined to raise awareness for the Connexion by means of a written prayer submitted to the Methodist newspaper, the *New Dimension* (2007: 3). The prayer was on 'Discovering the motherhood of God'. The purpose behind the prayer was to enable Methodist readers to discover that God is beyond gender and to invite readers to dialogue with them.

Although the learners raised their own awareness regarding the motherly nature of God, it is vital that the Church as a whole addresses this issue in different ways. An example is reflected in the *Faith and Life* group study booklet, which was available to all MCSA members. I concur with the writer that 'just because God is God, ... [God] cannot be bound by any limitations imposed by human minds' (Faith and Life 1991: 62).

The learners' discussions reminded me of my own seminary years. I remember my colleagues' rejection of the idea that God is not 'father' in a true sense. In arguing this 'fact', they supported their views by using the prayer that Jesus taught his disciples, when he said, 'Our Father' (Matthew 6: 9) as evidence that God is male. Zondi, one of the Lay Church leaders living with HIV, stated her uneasiness and struggle regarding the 'concept of a male and white God'. In her reflection she indicated that 'it was not easy to share my problems because such a God could not understand what

I was going through. But the God I now relate to is more like a woman – a caring person who listens, who is gentle, who loves me unconditionally and is always with me. So when things are difficult I know that God will always be at my side' (Zondi 2002: 34). There are many women like Zondi in our churches and hence it is vital for preachers of the Word to use inclusive language from the pulpit.

The traditional view of understanding God in sexist terms does not consider the fact that in Ruether's words, 'all language for God is metaphorical and not literal' (Ruether 1985: 8). Neither does it take seriously the fact that these are just metaphors, as pointed out by Mokhutso in his academic report on 'Trinity from a feminist perspective'. It does not seem to be appreciated that these metaphors are themselves influenced by a patriarchy which most men still believe to be the 'truth' about God (Mokhutso 2007: 8). These issues are especially noticeable in some hymns that are sung in the College Chapel and the exclusive language in many liturgies. They manifest also in prayers, Bible readings and sermons that are preached with sexist illustrations and jokes that belittle women.

In this paper the following will be presented:

1.   The rationale behind the course as outlined by TEE College.

2.   The challenge and impact of the course as perceived by those who registered for it at JWC.

3.   Learners' views on how the Bible has been misused in relation to marginalised women and how the Bible can be used to empower women as it is read through women's eyes.

4.   Learners' fears about making changes in local congregations and circuits in the light of the implications of the course.

5.   Concluding theological reflection.

'READING THE BIBLE THROUGH WOMEN'S EYES' (TEE COURSE 7/6378)

The course has been designed for distance education by TEE College in order to provide people with skills for ministry. It is an elective course for those studying towards the Diploma and/or Degree in Theology. The reason for reading the Bible through women's eyes is highlighted in the following statement from the course introduction: 'the Bible was written by men from a man's perspective. However the message of the Bible is not just for men, but also for women. If women are to be empowered and built up through reading the Bible they need to read it from their own perspective and to discern the andocentric nature of the text' (TEEC 2005: I). The course offers different skills and methods of reading the Bible, in particular reading behind the text, reading the text itself, and reading in front of the text.

Although scholars tend to choose a specific mode of reading with which they are comfortable, I believe there are advantages to using all three. For instance, in order for one to read the Bible critically, one needs to use all three modes, as all three highlight a different aspect of the Bible. According to West, 'behind the text' reading emphasises 'the historical and sociological context of the Bible'. The text itself stresses 'the literary and narrative context of the Bible', while reading 'in front of the text' emphasises the 'thematic and symbolic context of the Bible' (West 1993: 27).

THE CHALLENGE AND IMPACT OF THE COURSE, AS PERCEIVED BY THOSE WHO REGISTERED FOR IT AT JWC

John Wesley College Kilnerton

A word about the College where the learners did this course: Kilnerton became the site of the revival of John Wesley College when the Federal Theological Seminary (FEDSEM) was closed at the end of 1993. JWC in

Kilnerton was then opened in January 1994. In 2000 the Department of Theology and Religion at Rhodes University was also closed and, for the first time in the history of the Methodist Church of Southern Africa (MCSA), all student ministers had to be sent to one centre for residential theological education.

The course as perceived by those who registered for it at JWC

An interesting thing about the group doing the course was that there were 5 females and 6 males, which ensured lively discussions in class. 2007 was the first time that the College registered learners for the course. It has been disappointing to discover that, prior to this, very few learners, including women, had registered for this course, even though women are in the majority in the church. I would have hoped that learners would see a need for, and understand the importance of, the course for their preaching and teaching ministries. Khumalo reflected on the national statistics for 2005 in defining the challenges that women face:

- 1 in 5 women will be a victim of rape/attempted rape in her lifetime.

- 1 in 3 will have been beaten, coerced into sex or otherwise abused, usually by a family member or an acquaintance.

- Often the perpetrators go unpunished.

- Each year, hundreds of thousands of women and children are trafficked and enslaved; millions more are subjected to harmful practices.

- Violence kills and disables as many women between the ages of 15 and 44 as cancer.   http://www.unfpa.org/swp/2005/eng/cha7/index.htm (Khumalo 2008: January Seminar)

The above statistics call readers of the Bible to read and interpret the Bible, not only through male lenses but also from a feminine perspective. I concur with Fiorenza (2001: 90) that biblical interpretations need to take women's struggles seriously. Women who are reading the Bible must be prepared to interpret what they are reading from their own perspective without being locked into male doctrinal assumptions.

Challenges and impact of the course on the class of 2007

Challenges
In response to one of the assignments where the learners were required to prepare a Bible study for abused women, it is of interest to note that in general there is an assumption that ministers, whether ordained or on probation, have the skills to plan and to facilitate biblical studies in any and every context. My experience was that almost all the learners, both female and male, found themselves hugely challenged in planning for the task, not least in choosing a Biblical text that was relevant for abused women, and then having to run the Bible study themselves. According to Mokhutso, though he had 'read books on feminist theology' the challenge of the task lay in linking theory and praxis. The main challenge was 'to prepare the Bible study for the abused women' and the realisation that in future he may have to do so in a real situation proved a turning point in his thinking. The impact of the course on Mokhutso came to a head when he had to prepare a liturgy for a healing service for the abused women (Mokhutso 2007: 7).

In Cemela's reflection, the challenge was to design a Bible study that would enable women to 'break the silence' and the impact at the end was evident in an eagerness on her part to facilitate Bible studies for women in the Church. For Mofokeng, the challenge was personal in that she stated a need 'not to sit back and be silent as a women on issues of violent abuse, but to intervene and motivate women to seek help' (Mofokeng 2007: 10). As with Plaatjie, who facilitated workshops for grassroots women, these women student ministers discovered that they had a very poor self-image and needed to be empowered themselves (Plaatjie 1997: 8). This makes me believe that if women preachers are to be relevant, and to be able to preach sermons that will make a difference in the lives of other women, they need to do courses of this nature.

In addition, the other challenge that Mokhutso reflected in his work was that women who have been empowered by this tool of reading scripture through their own lenses, would be able to stand against patriarchy and challenge it (Mokhutso 2007: 2). Similarly, Malinga says that women leaders in the Church need to speak out (Malinga 2002: 5). Both of them are encouraging women not to internalise oppression but to stand up for what they believe. I concur with Hopkins (1999: 197), who says that 'the church should encourage women to love themselves more. The more they take care of themselves and are not servants to or dependent on men, the more they will be able to develop more healthy situations. ... Whatever happens, the black woman will be there to take care of the situation, or clean up after everybody else, or sacrifice her life, body, health, pleasure, job, and ideas for husband, children or the Church to feel better'. In most reports to our district synods, the work done by our mothers in the women's organisations (Manyano) requires of them to take care of themselves. My concern is that, in these synod reports, there is not much written about attendance at courses which empower women, nor about sending those in leadership on courses that would make a difference to the lives of all.

LEARNERS' VIEWS ON HOW THE BIBLE HAS BEEN MISUSED IN RELATION TO MARGINALISED WOMEN AND HOW THE BIBLE CAN BE USED TO EMPOWER WOMEN AS IT IS READ THROUGH WOMEN'S EYES

Learners' views on how the Bible has been misused in relation to marginalised women

According to Mofokeng, the two creation stories in Genesis 1 and 2 have been used to oppress women. Mokhutso supports this view by quoting West: 'This patriarchal perspective of women is theologically legitimated by male reading of the creation story (2: 13–15), and this reading has dominated thinking in the Church for centuries'. (West 1993: 53)

In support of West, Mokhutso states that the whole act of oppression and disempowerment is due to misinterpretation of this creation story, by the church, society and men (Mokhutso 2007: 4). In his view, 'the word "man" has always been translated as male and therefore oppressing women, making them feel inferior and also making "us" feel the second best from

God, i.e "not that important"'. Mofokeng continues to claim that this interpretation of the Bible has been taken for granted in patriarchal societies; that men will be head over all persons, including children and slaves (Mofokeng 2007: 9). It is a source of dismay that many readers of the Bible still read the Bible through this patriarchal lens. It is unbelievable to me that the oppression of women in the ancient Near East under patriarchy is still being experienced in some of our societies today. In the ancient Near East the status of women was very low. As LaCocque puts it, 'She was "in the care", first of her father or elder brother, then of her husband' (LaCocque 1990: 7).

Concerning the discrimination against women in the Church, Malinga states that people 'used the Bible and Christian theology' to justify their behaviour. Even though 'her denomination has accepted the calling of women to lead congregations as ordained ministers', her question is: 'What happened to the Methodist Church since women started playing this leadership role? Is there any transformation taking place? ... Many Methodist Christians ... have accepted and integrated into their self images the stereotypes and definitions that patriarchy places on men and women' (Malinga 2002: 3–4).

Mofokeng believes that 'gender oppression against women is a sin because it isolates humans from each other and from God'. After completing the course, Mofokeng indicated that reading the Bible through the eyes of women 'has been liberating'. She continues in saying that through this way of reading 'I reconnected with the God that we all worship, God saw my broken heart, my wounded histories and saw my need'.

The learner's views on how the Bible can be used to empower women as it is read through women's eyes

In his response on how he can use the Bible to empower women to challenge patriarchy, Mokhutso chose Genesis 1: 27 which he argues 'speaks of both male and female being created in the Image of God'. He then continues to indicate how he would go about empowering women through the text by teaching them that they are of value to God. I found his intentional interpretation of this text very empowering. The written text itself is not entirely gender sensitive. The language used is very exclusive. For instance, the text reads thus: 'So God created "man" in "his" own image, in the image of God "he" created "him" male and female'. This English rendering of the text uses very exclusive language and is still about the image of God first to men and then to women. As a third-language English speaker, there is no way I can understand that 'he' implies 'she', even though English speakers argue that 'man' includes woman. I concur with Dube that in the Setswana translation, the text is truly inclusive. Dube says: 'the book of Genesis presents Modimo as creator of the Universe and humanity (Genesis 1–2)'. She then continues to write verses 26–27 of the text that Mokhutso chose. My interest is in verse 27: 'Me Modimo oa tlhola motho mo chwanon ea ona tota, oa mo tlhola mo chwanon ea Modimo; oa ba tlhola nona le tshadi'. As Dube points out, in some English translations, 'humankind' is still rendered with the gender specific 'man' (Dube 2001: 89).

Like Dube and Mokhutso, Outler (ed) states that in Wesley's sermons on the image of God, the focus is on both male and female. Yet, curiously, he himself outlines his points as follows:

1. How man was made in God's image;

2. How he lost that image and

3. How he may recover it (Outler 1991: 14–15).

As someone for whom English is a third language I failed to feel included in his work. Unlike Dube, Outler chooses to use a translation that does not include women: 'So God created man in his image'. However, we must note that Outler in his introductory comment has highlighted Wesley's views in an inclusive manner. In the three stages of his argument he has pictures of a complete process from 'the original perfections of the *imago Dei* in Adam and Eve, to the state of the fall and destruction of this God's image. God through God's mystery of grace, promised to restore "defacement" of that image' (Outler 1991: 13). In other words, the process of perfection and restoration included both male and female. Hence, the fall and destruction of that image, which God has promised to both genders, is restored. This is the God that I believe in, who restores all his creatures regardless of their gender.

Applying the modes of reading and understanding the Bible, Makhudu's reading of 1 Corinthians 11: 2–16 was, first, an understanding of the socio-historical background of the text in order for her to understand the author's purpose. In applying the views reflected in her course workbook, she indicated that the context is different from today in that 'in first century Greece, dress for men and women was apparently very similar except for women covering their head' (TEEC 2005: workbook 4). Hence, she believes that in her present context she should not cover her head in church because she would be following the teachings of those who have misused the Bible for a long time (Makhudu 2007: 4, 6). This paradigm shift, as expressed by Makhudu, is similar to the experience of women who have been exposed to the contextual reading of the Bible. In his book, West refers to the work of both Sibeko and Haddad, in their discovery pertaining to some young Methodist women in Sobantu during a Bible study discussion, on Mark 5: 25–34, in which they 'choose not to take Holy Communion when they are menstruating'. Some of these women were possessed by an idea that they experience less power during this time of the month (West 1999: 167).

According to West, 'the facilitators (Sibeko and Haddad) acknowledge that it would be arrogant to suggest that these women readers have been definitively transformed and empowered through this particular reading of the text. There are ... tentative indications that a process of transformation has begun from their reading of this text' (West 1999: 165). The Contextual Bible study method, like the impact of the course as expressed by Makhudu, empowers women to question issues that are oppressive to them but have been accepted in our society as a part of culture.

LEARNERS' FEARS ABOUT APPLYING THE SKILLS LEARNED FROM THE COURSE

The learners' reservations about applying the skills and principles learned related to concerns that the MCSA (members of the church including senior ministers) was not ready for this way of reading the Bible. As all learners in this class were black, doubts as to whether they could be instruments of change were solely based on their past experiences as members in these black Societies and Circuits.

Their fears drew attention to the fact that, although women are in the majority in the Church, the majority of *preachers* are male – and in many societies, male preachers are given preference over females. These male preachers are reading the Bible from their male-dominated perspectives and tend to use illustrations that are not female sensitive. They also noted the fact that even women preachers still tend to read the Bible through male lenses. I tend to agree with them, because without training and a willingness to use the skills learned, it is impossible for readers of the Bible to read the text differently from the way they are accustomed to doing.

For example, I know that I myself used to read the Bible as a woman using a male lense, as this was the only way that I had been exposed to. The paradigm shift for me only happened during my university training and through my work with communities organised in a different way under the then Institute for the Study of the Bible (ISB) (Sibeko & Haddad 1997: 86). I believe that all preachers should be encouraged to register for this or a similar course, or their traditional way of reading the Bible will continue to exclude the majority of their hearers.

There are also other relevant resources that can assist those who are in training, and workshops that can be run for those who have completed their formal studies (Buckenham 199: 5). The current reality in our Church, according to Samdaan, is that in the MCSA there is a 'membership of about 2 million in Southern Africa, where women make up the majority (approximately 70 %) of our worshippers, yet the number of women in strategic leadership positions (Superintendents, Bishops, Connexional Unit posts, etc.) is less than 20 %' (Samdaan J 2007: 3). This reality calls for readers of the Bible in the MCSA to read the Bible differently. Reading the Bible through women's eyes can be an eye opener, especially for some black congregations within the MCSA. In some of these, traditionally women have not been allowed to preach from the pulpit, as this goes against culture and a literal reading of the text. Surely we need to reach the point in the church where 'Christian women ... Speak, sing, pray ... perhaps even debate' (Clouse 1989: 25).

Finally, in my introduction I mentioned that the discussions of the 2007 learners reminded me of FEDSEM years. As students we (three women students, together with a few supportive male colleagues) were exposed to different theologies, which included feminist theology. Like the 2007 learners who were afraid to implement the skills acquired, applying in Circuits what we had learned was very challenging. Often I would be branded a Feminist, a label which would be used with negative, almost un-Christian connotations. During meetings or at Synods where the Chair would use exclusive, sexist language, I would offer a reminder that women were present in the meeting. Some colleagues would reprimand me during breaks and insinuate that I was showing disrespect to the Chair. Those in the majority in these meetings, those in what Rieger refers to as the 'centre', were apparently comfortable with the language used. The voices of the marginalised, the 'silent voices' (words of the Presiding Bishop of the MCSA to the Connexional Executive, 2006), or those on the 'margins' (Rieger 2003), will always be forgotten.

Indeed, to use Rieger's words, 'when people from the margins want what everybody else wants, the centre pick up steam and thus may grant some justification to their concerns' (Rieger 2003: 17–20). I believe it is high time for those on the 'margins' to take their place so that those in the centre can be influenced by their views and so facilitate change. Skills obtained in reading the Bible using different models have enabled me to read the Bible from perspectives other than what I had been used to, skills I still use in my work with marginalised communities (West 1999: 26).

Reading the Bible through women's lenses has enabled me to be contextual, especially on special occasions such as Women's Day, Mother's Day and the 16 Days of Protest against violence against women and children. This way of reading has also empowered me to read unfamiliar texts, and this has led to new insights for me. The heart of the challenge has always been that of *exclusion* and has resulted in me becoming somewhat unpopular at times. Yet I believe that in order for women in the Church to feel included, women in leadership should not bother about whether or not they are popular. According to Malinga, 'in order to bring transformation, women leaders, like myself, need to insist on being themselves ... they do not need to imitate male leadership' (Malinga 2002: 5). I believe that, being a follower of Christ, I am called to turn tables upside-down and leave no stone unturned for the sake of transformation.

I believe that women need to speak out continually about views that keep on delaying the process of change. For instance, it is important to state that women are *still* made to feel inferior through the words, teachings and theologies that are prevalent today. I am of the mind, along with Keane, that the Early Church Fathers had already canonised an andocentric approach. What is more, the influence of their teaching is still being felt today (Keane M 1988: 4). The learners in their work were asked to write about views that the Early Fathers had concerning women, and the following emerged:

1. John Chrysostom said the following about women: 'Among all the savage beasts none is found to be so harmful as women.'

2. John Damascene continued by saying 'woman is a sick she-ass ... a hideous tapeworm ... the advance post of hell.'

3. Augustine of Hippo wrote: 'a woman apart from a man is not in the image of God, whereas a man apart from a woman is.'

4. Origin (AD 185–225) said: 'What was seen with the eyes of the creator is masculine, and not feminine, for God does not stop to look upon what is feminine of the flesh'. Mokhutso added that Origin heard this saying 'it is not proper for a woman to speak in Church, however admirable or holy what she says may be, merely because it comes from female lips' (Mokhutso 2007: 14 Ronald Dart, www. abcog.org retrieved 04/05/07).

5. Epiphanius (AD 315–403) stated: 'the female sex is easily seduced, weak, and without much understanding.'

6. Cyril of Alexandria (AD 376–444) said that because Mary Magdalene did not immediately recognise Jesus after His resurrection, 'Somehow the woman [Mary Magdalene], or rather the female sex as a whole, is slow in comprehension' (Ronald Dart, www.abcog. org retrieved 04/05/07)

7. Gregory: 'In Holy Scripture [the word] "woman" stands either for the female sex (Galatians 4.4) or weakness.'

The 2007 learners in this course discussed their reflections in class on the influence of these Early Fathers as they contributed to the misuse of the Scripture to oppress women. Reflecting on their comments during the class discussions confirmed my own feelings of unhappiness as I prepared for the class. I recall, from the comments of both male and female learners, frustration, anger, irritation, annoyance, disappointment, and more. In Mo-

---

fokeng's words, the Early Fathers' words 'are all in the past [and] women's voices must be heard!' (Mofokeng 2007: 11) With a different and strong tone, Mokhutso went so far as to claim that teaching about the Early Fathers had contributed to the abuse of women in the Church. Their teaching as 'great theologians contributed immensely in our Christian foundations' (Mokhutso 2007: 15). It is disappointing for me to note that Methodist theologians like Carder, speaking of Wesley's model of theological grounding, point out that although 'the Bible was its primary authority in matters of faith, nonetheless tradition, especially as expressed by the early church fathers, was also important' (Carder 1998: 23)

When it comes to matters of exclusion, the misuse of the Bible by some to exclude others, and being afraid to stir things up and make a difference, the only way real change can come is through a change of heart. It becomes a matter of personal spirituality. Hence, I share Rieger's opinion that all people will be transformed and at peace with one another, regardless of 'isms', as all partake around the Holy Communion table. He puts his views as follows:

> The Methodist tradition of the open communion table provides another reference point for a new theology and church. Holy Communion is not the place where the pious few meet in a safe retreat from the world. It is rather the place where people touched by God's grace seek to be forgiven and to live in peace with one another. (Rieger 2003: 25)

This implies, again according to Rieger, that encountering the presence of God around the Lord's table is 'closely tied to making peace with one another – something that cannot happen without those people who have suffered at times a veritable warfare along the lines of race, class, and gender' (Rieger 2003: 26). It is through the Lord's table that, for me, exclusivist sermons and interpretations of the Bible by theologians and preachers of the Word can be challenged and changed.

BIBLIOGRAPHY

Baker K, Burdrick D, Stek J, Wessel W, & Youngblood R 1984. *The NIV Study Bible*; Genesis 3. Zondervan

Bird, P A (ed). *Reading the Bible as women: Perspectives from Africa, Asia, and Latin America*. Atlanta: Semeia.

Byamugisha G, Steinitz L Y & Zondi P (eds) July 2002. Journeys of faith: Church-based responses to HIV and AIDS in three Southern African Countries, in *Women inspired by the Bible*. TALC

Buckenham, K (ed) 1999. *Violence Against Women: A resource Manual for the Church in South Africa*. Pietermaritzburg Agency for Christian Social Awareness

Carder, K L 1998. What difference does knowing Wesley make? in Maddox RL (ed) *Re-thinking Wesley's theology for contemporary Methodism*. Nashville: Abingdon

Clouse, B & Clouse R G (eds) 1989. *Women Ministry for Views: Let your women keep silence*. Library of Congress, USA

De Gruchy J W, Villa-Vicencio C, Cloete G D, Mosala I J (eds). March 1988. *Journal of theology for Southern Africa: A woman ought not to teach*. London: World Microfilms Publications

Dube M W, (ed) 2001. *Other ways of Reading: African Women and the Bible: Reading From the Translated and Gendered Modimo*. Library of Congress, USA

Dube M W, & Njoroge N J, (eds) 2001. *Talitha Cum! Biblical Metaphors of God*. Pieter-maritzburg: Cluster Publications

Feorenza, E S, 2001. *Wisdom Ways Introducing Feminist Biblical Interpretation: An Emancipatory Grassroots Democratic Ethos*. New York: Orbis Books

Ferguson S B, Wright D F, & Packer J I, (eds) 1988. *New Dictionary of Theology: Church*. Library of Congress, England

Fewel, D N & Phillips, G A, 1997. *Semela: an experimental journal for biblical criticism: Textual Excess And Reading*. Scholars Press, USA

Hopkins, D N, 1999. *Black Theology of Liberation; Womanist Theology*. Maryknoll: Or-bis books

Keane, M 1988. Women in the theological anthropology of the Early Fathers, in a *Journal of theology for Southern Africa* No. 62

Khumalo, B 2007. Dealing with diversity in our local Churches. Unpublished paper, January Seminar Gauteng

Malinga, P 2002. Women in Church Leadership: Co-option or transformation? in *Women in God's image – celebrating women's ordination*. No. 8, April 2002

Outler A C, & Heitzenrater R P, (eds) 1991. *John Wesley's sermons: The Witness of the Spirit*. Library of Congress, USA

Rieger J, & Vincent J J, (eds) 2003. *Methodist and Radical: Moving the Center*. Library of Congress, USA

Rieger J, & Vincent J J, (eds). *Methodist and Radical: Rejuvenating a Tradition*. Nashville: Kingswood Books

Reuther, R R 1985. *Womanguides: Gender Imagery for God/ess*. Library of Congress, USA

Oosthuizen, C. August 2006, First Ordained Methodist Woman Minister, in *Dimension* Vol. 36, No. 8

Samdaan, J J 2008. Establishment of an integrated and holistic Women's Ministries Division. An Unpublished paper prepared for the office of the Presiding Bishop. Johannesburg

Seitz, C R (ed) 1990. *The Feminine Unconventional: The status of women in the Near East and in Israel*. Library of Congress, USA

Sibeko M, & Haddad B 1997. *Reading the Bible as women: Perspectives from Africa, Asia, and Latin America*. Atlanta: Semeia

Wamue G, & Getui M (eds) 1996. *Violence Against Women: Women & Church Leadership*. Nairobi: Action Publishers

West, G O 1993. *Contextual Bible Study*. Pietermaritzburg: Cluster Publications

West, G O 1999. Remembering Rizpah: Rizpah 'Re-membering us', in *The Academy of the Poor*. Sheffield: Academic Press Ltd

FROM SANCTUARY TO STREET

In search of an African Methodist liturgical theology

John van de Laar

Time and space, birth and death, seasons and changes, love and justice – all of these things and more are contained and expressed in the worship life of the church. From the very beginning, at the heart of Methodism has been its gathering together – its music, its preaching, its celebration of the sacraments, its prayers and liturgies. Right from the start, the thinking and learning of Methodists has been developed through the worship life of the church. In this sense, the Methodist Church is, and always has been, a church of liturgical theology.

UNDERSTANDING LITURGICAL THEOLOGY

The word liturgy, or *leitourgia* in Greek, comes from two words – *leitos* meaning 'the people' or 'the public', and *ergon*, meaning 'to do' or 'to work'. Thus, 'liturgy' simply refers to 'a work of the people' or 'a public work'. While the word did not originally have a religious connotation, it has, over time, come to refer specifically to religious actions. In common use, this meaning has been narrowed still further to refer specifically to the work of gathering as a religious community for worship (see Benedict 2007: 14). Liturgical theology, then, is the theological thinking that flows from our experience of, and reflection on, the worship life of the church.

For liturgical theology to make sense, we also need to understand what we mean by the word 'worship'. This is no easy task, since worship is difficult to define. It is understood in a variety of ways by different people, and is impossible to separate from other activities in the life of the church or its people. Nevertheless, there are two main ways to grasp what we mean when we talk about the worship life of the church. The first is to reflect on how worship might be defined. While there is no shortage of definitions in the writing of liturgists and theologians, I remain convinced that the most helpful definition is the oft-quoted one written by William Temple (Archbishop of Canterbury 1942–44):

> To worship is to quicken the conscience by the holiness of God, to feed the mind with the truth of God, to purge the imagination by the beauty of God, to open the heart to the love of God, to devote the will to the purpose of God.

This definition expresses two important truths about worship: firstly that worship is not primarily about style or form but about an encounter with the divine that touches and changes the heart, and worship is expressed in the business of living not just in the weekly gathering.

The second way we can begin to understand what worship is is to explore what the church actually does when it gathers for worship. The scriptures offer clear indications of structures and activities that were inherently part of the worship life of Christians. Over the centuries, these structures have changed in style and form, but their basic character has remained surprisingly stable. They are found in every denomination and every community, although how they are expressed may vary greatly. These structures include:

- the setting aside of specific times and places for the community to gather;
- the reading of, and preaching from, the scriptures;
- the sharing in the sacraments;

- the celebration of rites of passage (weddings, funerals, confirmation etc.);

- the addressing of pastoral needs (confession, forgiveness etc.).

When these activities are placed alongside Temple's definition, we find a helpful framework for understanding what worship is. In worship, what we do, what we experience and how we think are brought together in such a way that we sense God connecting with us and forming us, and we are inspired and challenged to live our lives in accordance with the divine purpose. Liturgical theology, then, is the work we do to understand and explain the practice, experience and thinking of worship (see White 1990: 21–51 for a more detailed discussion on understanding Christian worship).

I am reminded of a Harvest Festival service that was celebrated in the church where I was working as a minister some years ago. The whole church had come together for the worship, and children were strongly in evidence in the sanctuary. During communion, the children were invited forward with their parents, and, before receiving the sacrament, they were given the opportunity to place food on the communion table to be distributed after the service to needy communities. One moment in this service stood out for me. As a young mother knelt at the front with her eyes closed, waiting to receive the bread and wine, her son, a toddler, stumbled over to the table and placed a can of food alongside the other offerings. As he stumbled back to his mother I thought to myself, *how little his mind must understand of all this, but how much his heart must have been formed by it.* This is the gift of liturgical spirituality and, when reflected upon, of liturgical theology.

THE LITURGICAL THEOLOGY OF AFRICAN METHODISM

While there are many sources of theological reflection in the Methodist Church, there can be no question that Methodism has always been formed and shaped by its experience of worship. John Wesley was deeply aware that the music of the people called Methodists should be both an authentic expression of worship and a way to teach and preserve the theology of the church. This is clearly demonstrated by his words in the preface to the 1780 Methodist hymn book:

> In what other publication of this kind have you as distinct and full an account of Scriptural Christianity? Such a declaration of the heights and depths of religion, speculative and practical? So strong cautions against the plausible errors, particularly those that are most prevalent? And so clear directions of making your calling and election sure: for perfecting holiness in the fear of God? (Warren 1988: 17–18)

In the thinking of the Wesleys, there was a strong connection between the quality of Methodist worship and the quality of Methodist theology. When they gathered as a community, the Methodist people were learning and doing theology. When they sang, prayed and received the sacraments, they were engaged in theological activity as much as liturgical activity. Their theology formed their worship even as their worship formed their theology.

> Wesley had come to understand the power of the wedding of text and tune as the most vital way of celebrating and remembering faith, scripture, theology, and the task of social service. The hymns had become the 'theological memory' of the Methodist movement, and if the singing of them were imprecise and nonchalant, so would be the theology of the church. (Young 1995: 74)

Methodism, then, has a long tradition of liturgical theology. But nowhere is this tradition more important than in Africa. It is on this continent that liturgical theology finds a soul mate – in African spirituality. In Africa, the lines between sacred and secular are blurred, the community and the individual are inseparable, and all of life is engaged and expressed through song.

> Certainly in Africa music is, and always has been, central to people's lives. Rural people sing about everything in their experience. They find in the music of their community a natural

way to focus on whatever activity they are involved in. There are songs not only for praise, worship, love and grieving, but for planting, cultivating and harvesting; songs for beginning a journey, for building a house, for pounding grain, for the carpenter or the blacksmith. The songs made by pastoral people for their animals are legion throughout Africa. And every important event in the life cycle is formalised in singing, dance or drama. Life without this connecting fibre of music and movement is inconceivable. (Scott 2000: 9)

Thus the spirituality of Africa is a musical spirituality, and, while worship and music are not synonymous, the thought of a music-less spirituality is foreign to the African worshipper. In the light of this, I would suggest that a liturgical theology is not only an authentically Methodist theology, but also an authentically African theology.

THE VALUE OF AN AFRICAN METHODIST LITURGICAL THEOLOGY

If this is the case, what might a liturgical theology offer to the Methodist Church of Southern Africa in the twenty-first century? At root, a liturgical theology creates a connection between the experience and understanding of worship in the sanctuary, and the living out of that worship in a life of following Christ in every relationship, every interaction, every situation and every moment. When this connection is intentionally nurtured and expressed in the worship life of a church, the impact of that church on the surrounding community must be profound.

Essentially, what this all means is that what happens in the sanctuary is actually not about what happens in the sanctuary. Worship is about life. The worship service is simply a time and space that we set aside, free from distraction, to learn to recognise God's presence, to hear God's promptings and to understand God's purposes. This is in order that when we move back out into our normal routines and relationships, we can encounter God in every time and every person and every place. When this happens, worship becomes not so much something we do, but something we are, and the fragrance of our worship flows into our lives, transforming them into an ever-growing likeness of Christ. Conversely, a liturgical theology draws from the experience of worshippers in their daily joys and struggles – the experience of poverty or wealth, HIV/AIDS, crime, relationship break-down, grief, love, childbirth, celebration and achievement – and creates the environment in which life's journey can be placed under the spotlight of God's truth and action. In this sense, worship is a dialogue between the sanctuary and the street, between God and the worshipping community, between our experience in the sanctuary and our experience outside of it.

For many followers of Christ, the only theology in which they engage is their worship. For many, the only way they think or act theologically is through their activity in the sanctuary. For many the only theology they learn is that which is absorbed through the prayers, hymns and symbols of the liturgy. This means that it is crucial that the church creates worship experiences that facilitate the dialogue between the worship service and a lived spirituality. This dialogue is best maintained when worship is formed with five theological principles in mind.

APOCALYPTIC WORSHIP

In the vision of John the apostle in the last book of the Bible, we read:

> I, John, your brother who shares with you in Jesus the persecution and the kingdom and the patient endurance, was on the island called Patmos because of the word of God and the testimony of Jesus. I was in the spirit on the Lord's day, and I heard behind me a loud voice like a trumpet saying, 'Write in a book what you see and send it to the seven churches, to Ephesus, to Smyrna, to Pergamum, to Thyatira, to Sardis, to Philadelphia, and to Laodicea.' Then I turned to see whose voice it was that spoke to me, and on turning I saw seven golden lampstands ... (Revelation 1: 9–12a)

The apostle, in the ancient equivalent of solitary confinement on Patmos, chooses to be 'in the spirit' on 'the Lord's day'. It is not unreasonable to imagine that this was John's way of expressing that he was engaged in the act of worship on the day when he knew all Christians would be gathering to celebrate and worship the Risen Christ. In the midst of this private worship service, John finds himself carried away by a grand vision. The rest of the book, then, is the description of this revelation that came to John as he was in worship.

Our word 'apocalypse' comes from the Greek *apokalupsis* which means revelation. Hence the worship of John that day on Patmos was 'apocalyptic' – it was worship that revealed something. What was revealed is simply explained in the introduction to the book – it was the 'revelation of Jesus Christ' (Revelation 1: 1).

Here the scriptures here give us an indication of one of the primary purposes of the worship life of God's people. God longs to be known by men and women, and God is always seeking to make Godself known. The scriptures are the story of this self-revelation of God to humanity, and they reveal throughout that people often encountered God in the place and the act of worship. There is no reason that this should be any different for us today. While our revelations may be far less dramatic in form than that of a John or a Moses, they certainly need be no less significant in terms of their impact on our lives. The work of theology is to notice God's self-revelation, reflect on it and apply its truths so that we may live better lives according to God's plan and purpose. The work of worship is to open us to the revelation of God on which theology is based.

What the book of Revelation indicates is that in worship God seeks to give new understandings of God's nature, character and purposes. In the sanctuary, God seeks to reveal something of God's perspective on the world and its affairs. And in the liturgy, God offers resources that can be carried out into the world as we seek to live our worship in the midst of daily routine. Worship, then, is to be apocalyptic.

In order to allow this revelatory work of liturgical theology to happen, worship leaders, preachers and ministers are called to create an environment in which people are opened to God's revelation, and in which God's revelation may most easily be made known. While the initiative in revelation, as with all worship, lies with God, knowing that God is ready and willing to reveal Godself, we are able to craft worship experiences that allow this revelation to become clear and to be received by God's people. The following simple suggestions have been found to be helpful in allowing people to experience something of God's revelation in worship.

Worship becomes apocalyptic when we move beyond a purely cognitive, rational experience. It is easy in worship to focus on our heads – what we think and say, what we understand. There is a place for this (as will be seen later), but worship cannot end here. For worship to shift into a revelatory experience, it needs to be just that – an experience. Emotions, intuition, mystery, symbol, metaphor and all the senses need to become part of the worship experience. Our sacraments, the poetry of the liturgy, the symbols in our windows and banners, the parables of Christ and the images of our songs all help to move us into a deeper knowing, a whole-person encounter with God that opens us to new inspiration, new experience and new understandings of God.

When worship allows this revelation to happen, worshippers become used to recognising God's presence even in the most unlikely places. When that happens, the whole world becomes a different place. Our revelation of God calls us to protect the planet which is our home, because it is here that God is revealed in every creature and place. Our encounter with God in worship opens us to the encounter that happens whenever we face other people and we are able to understand and live the truth of Jesus' words: 'Truly I tell you, just as you did it to one of the least of these who are members of my family, you did it to me.' (Matthew 25: 40)

THERAPEUTIC WORSHIP

There is a tendency in some quarters to separate the pastoral work of the church and its liturgical work. However, when our pastoral theology and practice is informed by worship, we discover that these two aspects of the church's life are inseparably linked. Worship is, in fact, therapeutic.

In 1 Samuel 16: 14–23, King Saul is troubled by a 'tormenting spirit'. In order to provide relief to the king, the young man David is recruited into the king's service. Whenever the spirit torments Saul, David plays his music, and Saul feels better. This, of course, is the same David who became the great psalmist. It is reasonable to assume, then, that the music David played was the psalmody with which he was so familiar – perhaps even some of his own compositions. The picture that comes to us in this biblical story is of a worship that heals – therapeutic worship.

The Gospels make it clear that, in a religious climate in which sickness or disability was seen as a curse, preventing the victim from entering the place of worship, Jesus embraced the broken in body and mind, and brought them gently into God's presence. The worship life of the church, then, is a place in which the church can exercise its ministry of healing, creating in the sanctuary a place to bring our pain and brokenness, and find comfort and relief.

For worship to be therapeutic, the church needs a theology and a practice of worship that intentionally creates space for pain, grief and questions. Our worship is often filled with the vibrancy of celebration and triumph, and so it should be. However, our worship needs equally to be filled with the solemnity of mourning, and the gentleness of compassion.

If we are to be a therapeutic church, we will also need to reclaim the ministry of lament. This prophetic work is clearly seen in the ministry of Jeremiah. In Jeremiah 20: 7–9, the prophet cries out to God:

> O LORD, you have enticed me, and I was enticed; you have overpowered me, and you have prevailed. I have become a laughingstock all day long; everyone mocks me. For whenever I speak, I must cry out, I must shout, 'Violence and destruction!' For the word of the LORD has become for me a reproach and derision all day long. If I say, 'I will not mention him, or speak any more in his name,' then within me there is something like a burning fire shut up in my bones; I am weary with holding it in, and I cannot.

In other versions of this passage Jeremiah accuses God of 'deceiving' him (Good News Bible), 'misleading him' (New Living Translation) or even 'seducing' him (The Vulgate)! In this outburst of anger and questioning of God, Jeremiah finds release and comfort, and there is no judgement toward him expressed in the scriptures. It can be a tremendously liberating thing for people to bring their doubts, questions and disappointments into the sanctuary and find that God is able to receive them and offer comfort.

Another way that worship becomes therapeutic is when we make space in the church for those who are visibly broken and hurting. A friend of mine in England who is a paraplegic has, more than once, had the humiliating experience of being asked to leave a church building because her wheelchair was in the way. I suspect that few people found the worship there to offer much in the way of healing. In contrast, in one church where I served, there was an annual event for the local home for severely mentally and physically retarded young people to come and sing in a worship service. While the music was tuneless and out of time, the exuberance and joy on the faces of the singers as they sang 'Jesus Loves Me' ensured that there was not a dry eye in the church. On those days we recognised through this group of broken people that we were all broken and in need of healing, and we remembered that God is a God who heals, even when we are not cured. We experienced therapeutic worship, and we did theology together as we reflected on brokenness and wholeness through the singing of these young folk.

Therapeutic worship that brings us face to face with the comfort and compassion of Christ, must inevitably lead worshippers to be healers. I do not mean this in the sense that we lay hands on every sick person and pray that they be made physically whole (although some of us may indeed be called into this work). What I mean is that when we as worshippers experience the therapeutic touch of God, we cannot help but extend that touch to others, through visiting, comforting, caring and listening. Historically, the church was at the forefront of the healing sciences as the call to extend the therapeutic ministry that flowed from worship was answered by faithful people. Today, in a world wrestling with HIV/AIDS, cancer, TB, Avian Flu and other serious diseases, the ministry of worshippers who have felt the therapeutic touch of God is needed as much as ever.

DIDACTIC WORSHIP

The apostle Paul, writing to both the Ephesians and the Colossians, encourages them in their worship with these enigmatic words:

> Let the word of Christ dwell in you richly; teach and admonish one another in all wisdom, and with gratitude in your hearts sing psalms, hymns, and spiritual songs to God. (Colossians 3: 16)

> Do not get drunk with wine, for that is debauchery; but be filled with the Spirit, as you sing psalms and hymns and spiritual songs among yourselves, singing and making melody to the Lord in your hearts ... (Ephesians 5: 18,19)

In both of these passages, Paul highlights the power of the worship life of the church to teach. As God's people sing and pray, receive the sacraments and read the Scriptures, preach and listen, they are learning. For many of them, this is the primary, if not the only, way that their faith is formed and informed. And so there is a strong need for our worship to be didactic – worship that teaches. This means that there is a great theological responsibility that is carried by our worship services. As Wesley noted, if our worship is shallow or narrow, so will be the theology and the faith of our people.

The didactic work of worship most obviously requires careful thought and planning with respect to every element of the service, and the relationship between the elements. The words of songs and hymns, the preparation and delivery of public prayer and the demeanour and liturgical actions of the leaders all contribute to our understanding of our faith and our God, and so must be thought through carefully. In addition, teaching happens best when it is presented in ways that are engaging, interesting and entertaining, in the sense of holding the attention. This means that worship cannot afford to become 'rote' in which words or songs are repeated without thought. Old forms need to be revitalised and used in new, relevant and startling ways. Worship that is didactic engages the minds of the worshippers, leading them into new thoughts, new questions and new ideas of faith, God and life.

When worship is created with this didactic responsibility in mind, followers of Christ become lifelong learners, interested in the world and willing to explore it and question it. Faith is no longer something to defend against other religions or ideas. Rather it is the filter through which we engage all thinking and searching. Rather than be afraid of questions, we remember that Jesus loved to ask questions, and we embrace Christ's call for us to be always learning (see John 16: 13f).

KOINONIAC WORSHIP

Martin Luther King Jr was direct and to the point when reflecting on the worship life of the Church:

> At 11: 00 on Sunday morning when we stand and sing and Christ has no east or west, we stand at the most segregated hour in this nation. (From his speech at Western Michigan University, 1963).

It is an unfortunate reality that worship is often what most divides the Church. This is not a new phenomenon, however. Even Paul had his hands full trying to reconcile the Corinthian Church which was divided in their worship.

> Now in the following instructions I do not commend you, because when you come together it is not for the better but for the worse. For, to begin with, when you come together as a church, I hear that there are divisions among you; and to some extent I believe it. (1 Corinthians 11: 17–18)

The Church has long wrestled with differences in age, race, culture, gender, style, musical preference, personality, theology and practice, and many of these differences have caused great pain and deep rifts between various groups of Christ-followers. There is another possibility for our worship, though, expressed as an invitation by the Psalmist:

How very good and pleasant it is when kindred live together
in unity!

It is like precious oil on the head, running down upon the
beard, on the beard of Aaron, running down over the collar
of his robes.

It is like the dew of Hermon, which falls on the mountains
of Zion. For there the LORD ordained his blessing, life forev-
ermore. (Psalm 133)

When a community of worshippers is able to preserve their unity, their
shared life – *koinonia* in Greek – and express this in their worship, there is
a tremendous strength, blessing and joy that results. A liturgical theology
and practice that fails to take *koinonia* seriously is deeply flawed.

While worship can be expressed and experienced individually, the scriptures know nothing of a solitary spirituality. Even when alone in prayer, the
individual remains connected with the community of faith. This is why,
when teaching about prayer in the Sermon on the Mount, Jesus insists that
even in the privacy of a room alone, we should still pray '*Our* Father ...' (Matthew 6: 6–9). Any theology of worship that gives primacy to the individual's
experience of God or expression of devotion falls short of the biblical idea of
worship being primarily a shared activity. When we lose connectedness with
each other in our worship, not only does our theology fall into the straight-
jacket of individualism, but our relationship with God necessarily remains
one-dimensional and shallow. The scriptures make it clear that the *imago
dei* – the image of God – is revealed in every human being. Thus, when
we gather, we gain access to insights and experiences of God that are una-
vailable to us when we are alone. A healthy liturgical theology must have a
well developed ecclesiology – understanding of the church – and this strong
grasp of the nature and importance of the community, in turn, deepens and
enriches our worship and the theology which flows from it.

Part of the *koinonia* which is experienced in our worship is the connection with the Church of Christ universal and eternal. In Africa, the connection with the 'ancestors' is well known and those who have gone before
us in the faith – whom the book of Hebrews calls the 'great cloud of wit-
nesses' (Hebrews 12: 1) – are remembered and venerated. In addition, the

community of faith spreads across the globe and into every culture and denomination. When our worship can embrace the Church throughout the earth and throughout time, we begin to embrace a truly *koinoniac* liturgical life.

In 2001 I was asked, for the first time, to plan and lead the worship for Conference – the then biennial national decision-making body of the Methodist Church of Southern Africa. I was rather nervous as I accepted the position, and called a group of gifted liturgists and musicians together to help do this work. Each day of the Conference, we were to gather for about forty minutes of worship, ensuring that all of the different languages, musical styles and hymnodies of our church were equally included. After months of planning and long rehearsals, the Conference came together and the worship began. It took only a few minutes for me to realise that this team had managed to achieve something very special. Moving from organ to acapella to contemporary band to various combinations of them, praying and singing in at least six of the eleven official South African languages, shifting leadership from young to old, from black to white and from male to female and back again, this was the first experience of truly blended, multi-cultural worship that I had ever had. And the delegates were drawn into the worship together, dancing and singing with rapturous faces and exuberant voices. After one of the morning worship times, one of the delegates came up to me to say thank you. 'I felt like I was part of that scene in the book of Revelation where people from every tribe and language and people and nation are gathered around the throne of God,' he said.

What most surprised and inspired me about these times of worship, though, was the impact they had on the business of the meeting. The debates were somehow more cordial and less confrontational. The whole spirit of the Conference was one of joyful unity. The theology we had practiced and proclaimed in our worship was now being lived in the rest of our day.

KERYGMATIC WORSHIP

A relatively recent phenomenon in the history of the Church is the appearance, particularly in the United States of America, of so-called seeker-sensitive churches. These churches set aside specific times, usually their primary weekend services, to create an evangelistic event that draws those who do not regularly attend church. The presentation is usually incredibly slick and professional, utilising state-of-the-art multi-media and sound systems, and top quality musicians, actors and public speakers. The idea behind this movement is that the Church is competing with the professional entertainment industry for people's attention, and that this requires a high quality, entertaining presentation to be offered in order to bring people in so that they can hear the Gospel message. The format is usually 'presentation based' with little if any participation by the congregation, and what happens in these services is seldom referred to as worship, because the belief is that only Christians can really worship God. For this reason, 'worship services' for 'believers' are usually held at a different time – possibly mid-week.

While much good has been done by these churches in raising awareness of the Gospel mandate to 'make disciples' and while many people testify to life changing encounters with Christ through these churches, I remain disturbed by both the theology and liturgical practice of 'seeker-sensitivity'. Perhaps my primary concern is the dualism that is created between proclamation of the Gospel – what in Greek is called the *kerygma* – and the act of worship. The idea seems to be that worship and proclamation cannot mix and must be kept apart.

However, throughout the scriptures, both Old and New Testaments, there is a clear call to include the 'alien' and the 'foreigner' in the worship of God's people. There is no justification for the view that only Christians can worship, and there is no sense of dividing worship from proclamation. On the contrary, Paul, in writing to the Corinthian Church makes it clear that they must expect strangers to come into their worship and prepare accordingly:

> If, therefore, the whole church comes together and all speak in tongues, and outsiders or unbelievers enter, will they not say that you are out of your mind? But if all prophesy, an unbeliever or outsider who enters is reproved by all and called to account by all. (1 Corinthians 14: 23–24)

As Sally Morgenthaler writes in her ground-breaking book *Worship Evangelism*:

> Nowhere does Scripture say that seekers do not belong in worship. Nowhere does it say that seekers cannot be moved by observing God's interaction with believers. On the contrary, worship and evangelism are conspicuously linked throughout Old and New Testaments. (Morgenthaler 1995: 81)

I would go even further than Morgenthaler and assert that there is really no clear line between 'believers' and 'seekers'. Many so-called believers still feel as though they continue to have questions and doubts, and would still consider themselves seekers, even though they are deeply committed to Christ and to the church. On the other hand, many 'seekers' may not have prayed a specific prayer or attended a church regularly, but they have a deep faith and consider themselves to be believers. From the perspective of liturgical theology, kerygmatic worship – worship that proclaims the message of Christ – is equally important and necessary for the committed and the not-so-committed.

The worship life of the Church holds a tremendous opportunity for fulfilling the Great Commission. It offers the possibility of encounter with God, the invitation to gather with others who are seeking to live out their lives connected with their spiritual centre, and the chance to be influenced and transformed by time-tested and honoured truths. In this invitation, our worship, both in act and word, is kerygmatic.

Further, the worship of the church affords a unique opportunity to confront the values and norms of society where they conflict with those of the reign of God. In the prophetic ministry of justice and compassion, of confrontation of oppressor and comfort of oppressed, the worship life of the church is kerygmatic. By using language that is inclusive, by opening the door wide to any who would enter, by refusing to perpetuate in the sanctuary any injustices that bring pain and harm outside of the sanctuary, the liturgical life of the church speaks with a prophetic voice.

During the apartheid years in South Africa's history one of the most profound acts of protest that was performed by Methodists and other

Christians, was in choosing to worship together across the colour bar, even though this was legally forbidden. When white Christians journeyed illegally into black townships in order to worship together, or black Christians risked being accosted, searched or even arrested for coming into white areas to worship, the church was doing theology and proclaiming the *kerygma*. And when our worship challenges us to follow Christ daily in such a way that others are attracted to him, and to stand against the evil in the world, we know the we have heard the Gospel again as we have worshipped, and we find the strength and the guidance to live the Gospel in our lives.

FROM SANCTUARY TO STREET

The worship life of the church is all too often seen as an optional extra – a prelude to the real event which is the sermon (which should rather be considered as simply one element of the worship). For many the work of singing, praying, enacting, proclaiming and celebrating is a lesser work of the Church, fading away behind the more important functions of service, social justice and upliftment – the work, which in Greek would be called *diakonia*.

However, when a dualism is created between *diakonia* (service) and *leitourgia* (worship), both ministries are diminished. Worship without service is irrelevant and escapist, but service without worship is soulless and debilitated. When the two are brought together, the Church becomes a community of power and impact, of vision and creativity, of wisdom and practical contribution. The theology that is formed by, and informs, our worship is one that is apocalyptic, revealing God and God's purposes for the world to us again and again, and inspiring us to make God's glory known in all places, all people, all times and all circumstances. It is therapeutic, bringing God's comfort and healing to broken hearts, minds and bodies, both through the act of worship, and through the life that is lived because of worship. It is didactic, training the mind of worshippers to understand and explore the richness of God's truth, and inspiring us to make all of life a quest to discover God's mysteries in the world. It is koinoniac, bringing together all people in the act of worship, and leading us ultimately to embrace all of humanity as God's people. And it is kerygmatic, inviting all into the abundant life that Christ offers, and confronting all powers that would rob others of this life, whoever they may be. The sum of liturgical theology is a rich and transforming experience and understanding of worship which cannot help but lead us into deep and transforming engagement with the world – the work of *diakonia*.

This has always been the way of Methodism, as is evidenced by the two facets for which the original Methodists were most known – their work for social justice and compassion, and their music and worship. They are two sides of Methodist spirituality, Methodist theology and Methodist practice, and they can never be separated. In Methodism, and especially here in Africa, worship flows from the sanctuary to the street, sanctifying all of life. And life out on the streets ultimately leads us back into the sanctuary, where we bring our struggles and our joys to be transformed through encounter with God.

BIBLIOGRAPHY

Benedict, D T 2007. *Patterned by Grace*. Nashville: Upper Room Books.

Morgenthaler, S 1995. *Worship Evangelism*. Grand Rapids: Zondervan.

Scott, J 2000. *Tuning Into a Different Song*. Pretoria: The Institute for Missiological and Ecumenical Research.

Warren, J I 1988. *O For A Thousand Tongues*. Grand Rapids: Asbury Press.

White, J F 1990. *Introduction to Christian Worship*. Nashville: Abingdon.

YOUTH DEVELOPMENT IN SOUTH AFRICA

A psycho-spiritual perspective

Mogomotsi Diutlwileng

INTRODUCTION

Youth Development is the name given to an effort led by the democratic government of South Africa to empower young people to realise their full potential in the social, economic and political spheres of life and to play a role in building a better life for all. The democratic government of South Africa adopted a National Youth Development Policy Framework (2002–2007) as a guide for implementing youth development. This chapter will offer a critical theological reflection on the impact of youth development over the 2002–2007 period. The reflection will encompass all critical aspects but with special focus on the psychological and spiritual dimensions.

In an unpublished paper entitled 'Youth Work Curriculum, Training and Best Practices' delivered at the National Youth Development Practice Policy Conference of the Department of Social Development in February 2008, my assertion was that 'although great strides have been achieved in political emancipation and social consciousness, sadly, the education sys-tem, in particular the Youth Work curricula, have capacitated the youth just enough to make them a useful volunteer pool of economic slaves.' (Diutlwileng 2008: 1). This paper takes that discussion to a deeper level and shares a perspective on the negative impact that Youth Development has had on the psyche and spirituality of the youth when it failed to bring about the economic emancipation of young people.

Theologically, youth development affirms the question of human dig-nity as derived from the fact that humanity was created in the image of God. So the failure of youth development to grant young people economic liberation, and thus affirm their dignity, has devastating psychological and spiritual consequences. But more pertinently, it is the church's failure to take on the banner of youth development as a mission thrust that really creates a situation of disillusionment.

In this chapter we look at:

• The vision and strategic interventions of youth development;

• The theological basis for youth development;

• Failures of youth development;

• Psychological and spiritual damage;

• Youth development as a mission thrust.

THE VISION AND STRATEGIC INTERVENTIONS OF YOUTH DEVELOPMENT

The vision of Youth Development between 2002 and 2007 was to empower the youth to be meaningful participants in mainstream economic, social and political activities. Young people were recognised as critical partners in that process of their development, in that they were also expected to take responsibility in creating a better life for all. This effort was meant to redress the injustices and discrepancies of the apartheid era.

The first post-apartheid decade in South Africa saw young people com-prising a large proportion of the unemployed: 'The number of unemployed young people was 3.5 million. One third of all youth (18 million) lived in poverty, including 16 per cent as part of the ultra-poor, with the highest rates of poverty, and ultra-poverty, in younger ages of the youth category, amongst 18–24 year olds' (Status of the Youth Report 2005). The result of this situation is that up to today, this is hampering the ability of young people to live a fulfilling life, realise their potential and participate meaningfully in the social, political and economic mainstream activities of society. Yet Youth Development, as envisioned in the national policy framework, purported to be a tool to reverse this reality.

This raised young people's hopes for economic liberation. These hopes were authenticated by the establishment of the Umsobomvu Youth Fund and other enterprise development agencies of the state. The mandate of these agencies was to empower young people with skills that would enable them to penetrate the labour market and to fund and support youth enterprises. The National Youth Service Unit was mandated to mobilise youth, offer structured learning programmes, place youth in community-based service activities and channel them into labour market opportunities. This is a multi-million rand government programme that in its essence promised to speed up service delivery and address the economic quandary of thousands of young people. So, given all these programmes and initiatives born in the name of youth development, young people's high hopes of emancipation were not unfounded.

A THEOLOGICAL BASIS FOR YOUTH DEVELOPMENT

Essentially, youth development is about bread-and-butter issues, i.e. skills and economic participation. In this case, the theological cornerstone of youth development concerns the notion of human dignity. Young people, created in the image and likeness of God, have been endowed with the character to subdue and exercise stewardship over the created order around them. Human beings represent the crown of God's creation, as articulated in the psalmist's prayer of adoration: 'you made him a little lower than the heavenly beings and crowned him with glory and honour.' (Psalm 8: 6)

So, if a young person is unemployed, poor and unskilled, he or she will feel subdued by their circumstances and ruled by the conditions of their existence. This fundamentally strips a young person of the very thing that makes them human — having dignity, glory and honour.

Again, a young person has a Divine and natural inclination to need to work, to be in control of their life and be productive. There is ample New Testament evidence that God desires human beings to live fruitful and productive lives. A compelling principle emerges that it is not enough just to be alive but there is a need to be productive. Productivity gives evidence of being alive. Now, we can be productive in very many areas of our lives. But one very important area that reflects productivity and enhances one's glory is economic productivity. The profundity of this principle is more recognisable when theologising within a context of capitalism and globalisation. Young people experience a compelling pressure to be economically productive. If they are not able to do so, they feel a natural discontent and frustration because they are made to feel subhuman and often alienated from God. Fundamentally, therefore, youth development relates to questions of God-given human dignity, pride and honour.

In addition, youth development is ideally about a person doing community service and contributing to creating a better life for all. Thus it should be about people working together in their communities to help each other out of a situation of disgrace and indignity. As a person theologising from a context of and influenced by an African way of life, this kind of involvement in community life helps to keep an important value intact. It gives a person a sense of belonging. It is a powerful way of recalling, in a capitalist context which focuses on the individual, that 'I am because other people are.' Youth development holds a powerful element of rebuilding community life that espouses mutual benefit for all concerned.

FAILURES OF YOUTH DEVELOPMENT

The ideal of youth development reflects a great vision that has theological and moral backing. However, the practical implementation thereof leaves a lot to be desired, especially with regard to the economic emancipation of young people. Essentially, youth development was driven by government departments. Non-governmental organisations became involved as service providers to deliver on a particular government department's mandate. Inevitably, government departments each have their own service delivery mandate and priorities. Therefore, any programme in which they engage, including youth development programmes, will focus on and prioritise in terms of their own mandate. Youth were to be mobilised, offered skills training (relevant to whatever service they are required to render at that time), plunged into some kind of service and, after a contract period, normally one year, released into a life of unemployment once more.

Cases where young people were absorbed into positions in the government department represent a very insignificant number. Hence my contention that Youth Development has capacitated young people enough only to make them into a useful pool of volunteers for government programmes and purposes. In all fairness to the architects of Youth Development, I do not believe that it was a deliberate strategy to do that to young people. It is a situation that evolved when people were trying to perform their duties informed by their respective mandates, while at the same time trying to satisfy a policy that required that young people be empowered.

The National Youth Service Programme is another typical example where Youth Development was intended to help but ended up not meeting young people's needs. National Youth Service was identified as the most effective way of delivering the development of youth. The programme mobilised youth by the thousand, trained them and placed them in service areas in communities and at the end of the project facilitated their placement in job and further learning opportunities. The major problem of this programme was that, first, the programme trained young people in skills that were not necessarily scarce or prioritised. The skills offered were normally what the government needed young people to know for them to be able to assist in fast-tracking service delivery. Beyond the project, if the particular department did not absorb a young person, they were basically out on the street again.

Second, the exit strategy to facilitate the placement of youth in secured jobs or further learning opportunities, remains a continuous challenge. The departments cannot give a guarantee to all the participants that they will be employed. But what is even more debilitating is that once the project is over, the youth lose the stipend that they have been used to receiving for about eighteen months. Now, South Africa being the consumerist society that it is, with little if any saving, youth generate debts during the period of participation in the project because of their meagre income. When the project folds up, a young person is left with no income, in debt, poorer and more depressed. We then have the situation where young people hop from one government project to the next just so that they can have a continuous income, thus becoming economic slaves.

But the greatest failure of Youth Development is that it fails to transform the mentality and orientation of young people from seeking employment to creating employment. The reality of our economy is that job security is shrinking and increasingly new job opportunities are on a non-permanent basis. If Youth Development is going to be effective, it needs to create more entrepreneurs to create more jobs. In order for Youth Development to do that, we first need to dismantle a well established mental framework of 'study hard so you can find a good company to work for.' (Kiyosaki 2001: 20). This process of dismantling the employee mentality needs a concerted effort of education, reorientation and motivation by strategic people who have made great strides in business themselves and could serve as role models and mentors for youth. Instead, we got employees of government to tell young people that they must be employers ... 'and be like whom?' Eventually, money was given to people who had neither the skills nor the drive to be in business, and few grew into sustainable enterprises.

PSYCHOLOGICAL AND SPIRITUAL DAMAGE

When Youth Development was introduced, it created hope and excitement in young people. Young people who had qualifications hoped that they would then get secure jobs and be economically self-reliant. Excitement came from the fact that even those who did not get halfway through high school education would regain an opportunity to obtain skills and jobs. The prospect of a young person owning a business and employing others created great excitement. It was seen as an effective way to restore dignity and uplift the youth emotionally and economically.

However, the reality of Youth Development is that, first, it offered skills that were economically redundant, like training people to be administrators and counsellors. Second, it was incapable of creating secured jobs in the market for young people. Third, some of those who got funding to start enterprises did not survive the robustness of the business world. Basically, Youth Development took young people on a trip around the block, and raised hope and excitement, only to take them back to the same spot of helplessness and discouragement. During my own time as a Youth Development practitioner, in personal interaction with young people, it has become very clear to me that this has left young people with some devastating psychological scars.

Stress and depression

The failure of Youth Development to deliver left young people stressed and frustrated. Most of these young people were stressed because they had family responsibilities to fulfil. Some of them have children and siblings to take care of. Their ambitions, hopes and dreams were doused when they realised that they could hardly survive. And when they sensed being at an economic dead-end, it sent some of them straight into a state of depression.

Sadly, some of them could not take the stress and depression, felt helpless and hopeless, and were driven to suicide. Obviously, it is not that there was no hope or help, it is just that in their state of mind unemployment and dependency on others was just as good as being dead.

Self-image and self-esteem

In a capitalist country like South Africa where one's value in society is measured by material prosperity, being unemployed and poor can be brutal to one's self-image and self-esteem. When the reality of being economic slaves hit young people, some of them developed a negative self-image. This is to say, they viewed themselves in a negative light as if they were useless and worthless. In the face of their family responsibilities and expectations, some young people convinced themselves that they were irresponsible or stupid.

In their situation of desperation, depression and confusion, the youth compared themselves with other young people who were seemingly prospering. As a result, their self-esteem hit rock bottom. They started to doubt their intelligence, skills, gifts and talents. Inevitably, they entertained negative thoughts about themselves until those became part of who they were. As John Kehoe says, 'your subconscious mind will accept any thought about yourself that you regularly think, true or not, and that idea will eventually become part of your self-image' (Kehoe 1997: 86). As their subconscious absorbed those negative ideas of themselves some of them lost self-love. Sadly, when that happened, some young people resorted to crime, substance abuse and sexual promiscuity. This was done in an attempt to deal with the economic situation, to assert themselves and seek love outside themselves.

Spiritual damage

As a result of the overwhelming situation, young people tried to find meaning out of all this confusion. In a situation created by the failure of Youth Development to liberate them, youths sought answers from the faith realm. They felt as though God had ditched them, which reinforced their loss of self-worth. The big question became, 'If God is present and loves me, why am I in this dehumanising situation?' Again, 'If God loves all people equally, why is it that others prosper and I am lost in a swamp of poverty and indignity?' This caused these young people to doubt the power, love and care of God, which led to a breakdown in relationship with God.

But what was catastrophic was that, as these young people went down this lonely road, asking these crucial questions and playing the negative messages over in their minds, the church was complacent and went on with its 'business' ignorant of where the young folks were at. There was no positive alternative and no hope-restoring message or even an attempt to provide answers to the questions on these young people's minds. So, church became a useless institution in the lives of these wounded young souls. And when some of them abandoned the church and faith, the church rationalised and blamed the youth for being rebellious and lacking in faith.

However, the biggest crisis and the saddest thing was that the forces of darkness saw the confusion and the need in the youth and snatched them. When you talk to young people who were once caught up in the practices of Satanism, one common thread is that the agents of this evil practice lured them in with a 'promise' of material possessions. This highlights the fact that the question of economics is of foremost importance to young people and the Satanists know this.

The apartheid-era injustices and discrimination had a negative impact on the faith and orientation of young people. But the failure of Youth Development left young South Africans sad and sick.

YOUTH DEVELOPMENT AS A MISSION THRUST

In the light of the effects of the situation described above, I think the challenge is now upon the church to take youth development as a mission thrust. In terms of the four mission pillars identified by the Methodist Church of Southern Africa, youth development surely falls squarely within the scope of the Empowerment and Economic Development pillar. As I said earlier this is a question of the restoration of human dignity. But it is also a question of restoring confidence and hope in God and the church.

The Mission Unit, as the custodian of our mission strategy and priorities, needs to list Youth Development as a Key Performance Area and dedicate a Co-ordinator to focus upon it. This mission thrust must forcefully engage in entrepreneurial skills development, a life reorientation programme, a spiritual development programme and enterprise funding programme. We need to transform the frame of mind from that of a job seeker to job creator. To this end, an effective entrepreneur mentoring and coaching programme is absolutely crucial.

Now, part of the challenge for taking this direction might be finding the funds to support such a mission thrust. However, I believe we have not yet seriously made an effort to pull the church's money together, redirect income streams like the 'poor fund', review the assessment portfolio of organisations like our Women's and Men's groups, challenge business people and the growing middle-class sector within the churches, launch robust fundraising drives and establish strategic partnerships with government and other agencies. Furthermore, other creative initiatives like the Youth Economic Development Programme of the Limpopo District Youth Unit, need to be encouraged. This programme has established a church resource fund to support business initiatives of youth within the church.

However, before we can spend time and resources on training and funding of youth enterprises, we need to attend to the fundamental issues. Our youth development programme needs at the same time to address the problems at psychological, emotional and spiritual levels. We need to ensure that young people are motivated, have a positive attitude, self-image and self-esteem, and self-love. Otherwise, we will be throwing money and resources into a fast-flowing river that is tributary to the sea of waste. In business, success is realised primarily at a psychological level before it is outwardly manifested.

Spirituality must be the base for youth development. Jesus, in the story of the feeding of the five thousand in John 6, spells out to the crowd that they are looking for him, not because they saw miraculous signs but because he fed them with bread. We must be careful as the church not to attract people to us simply because they 'ate the loaves and had [their] fill' (John 6: 26b). Our programmes must be structured in such a way that our ultimate goal is for people to have a relationship with the Christ who offers the bread and not with the bread itself. There is a need to affirm the dignity of the youth and anchor their spiritual base through focused and intentional Spiritual Development programmes.

Capitalism and the church

As a church we need to face the fact that we are witnessing the reality of capitalism, which has very harsh and degrading effects on the poor of our society — of which the majority are young people. We need to realise that this economic system is not about to fade away in South Africa or in the global village. To stand on the periphery and complain to each other about the bad and negative effects of capitalism is not going to make it go away.

Therefore, I think the most responsible thing to do is to get into the play and bring in the God-factor as the hinge of practising capitalism. Beyond

Youth Development as a mission thrust, we need to develop an economics education programme. The essence of this programme will be, first, to heighten the knowledge of economics amongst faith communities. This will assist us in intelligently engaging other role players when we advocate for economic justice. Second, and most important, such a programme should infuse principles, values and Christ-like morality in believers so that in practising capitalism they exude these qualities until capitalism is influenced by them. I believe it is possible, and with faith and Holy Spirit-courage, we can influence and transform the world of economics 'for the healing of nations.'

Theologising in the context of oppression and apartheid led toward Liberation Theology and this theology helped us to appropriate God and Faith in a context of captivity. Now, in the new democratic dispensation, the greatest challenge is around development and economics. The Youth Development and the Economics Education programme as suggested above can lead us toward Development Theology. This envisaged brand of theology can be a tool in the hand of the church to dismantle the hold of economic servitude and lack of appropriate skills, and the negative psychological and spiritual effects on our young people.

CONCLUSION

Youth Development has raised the hopes and excitement of youth, but failed to give them genuine economic emancipation. In the process, it has left young people as economic slaves — stressed, depressed, suicidal, and with a very low sense of self-esteem, self-image and self-love. It has left youth in a spiritual jungle, lost, confused and vulnerable to the pull of the kingdom of darkness. On the other hand, youth development has a theological basis in raising the question of human dignity, glory and pride. It strongly affirms the role and responsibility of humanity to subdue and be stewards of creation. In redressing the problem, the church must take youth development as a mission thrust to skill, motivate and support youth. But fundamentally, our efforts must lead youth to a relationship with Christ. In addition, it would be responsible for the church to face up to the challenge of capitalism and engage in an Economics Education programme which will ultimately assist us to move toward a new brand of theology called Development Theology.

BIBLIOGRAPHY

National Youth Development Policy Framework 2002–2007

State of the Youth Report 2004 – Commissioned by Umsobomvu Youth Fund conducted by HSRC of South Africa

UYF Annual Report 2007

Diutlwileng, M 2008. *Youth Work Curriculum, Training and Best Practices – National Youth Development Practice Policy Conference of the Department of Social Development, February 2008*

Kehoe, J 1997. *Mind Power into the 21st century.* Zoetic Inc

Kiyosaki, R with Lechter, S L 2001. *Rich Dad Poor Dad.* Warner Books

EDITOR'S CONCLUSION – WHAT ARE WE THINKING?

I have no doubt that many of the ideas and concepts contained in the pages of this book have been challenging and stimulating. At the same time, however, I'm sure that there would have been some ideas with which you could not agree. That is the nature of diversity. Diversity is born out of difference. What is magnificent, however, about the people called Methodist in Southern Africa is that we have been wise and mature enough to hold our differences in loving tension with one another. We have learnt through the struggle of our own past that difference should never be a cause of separation or rejection. As a nation we have discovered that our diversity can be a gift. Differences in race, gender, age, and even theology, can lead to enrichment and growth.

Each of the authors who contributed to this volume has given us a tremendous gift. Many have spent hours poring over books and articles. Some have conducted interviews and travelled the 6 nations of our Connexion in order to sharpen their thoughts and test their ideas. The result is that you and I have something that we can call our own. This is some of 'what we are thinking', and it fills me with great hope for our Church and our nations. When I read these chapters I am proud to be a Methodist in Southern Africa!

As I read I was constantly struck by the passion of these ministers. Each one wrote with insight and commitment to the matters they had considered. What we have read stems from a deep sense of conviction grounded in the Gospel of Jesus Christ and the establishment of God's Kingdom.

In conclusion I would like to encourage you to consider a few points.

First, I would encourage you to get involved in forging the theology and policy of our denomination. Each of the issues discussed in this book has something to do with the way in which we do mission in the world. Let's not sit on the sideline as spectators; rather let's get into the fray and offer our best. Your opinions and ideas count! So please have the courage to make them heard.

Second, I would encourage you to be prayerful about the issues that we currently face in our context. Let us never forget that we are a people of faith who believe in a God who is powerful and loving. So let us be faithful to pray about the concerns and struggles of our people.

Third, I would encourage you to keep on developing your theology by reading and dialoguing with others. Theology should not be a static enterprise. It should rather be a dynamic process of discerning God's will and God's ways, and courageously trying to live in obedience to these. I would encourage you to try to understand the opinions of others, even those with which you disagree. Be prepared to have your own ideas and beliefs challenged – you may just learn something new in the process!

Finally, I would encourage you to be practical about your theology. All good theology is ultimately practical. It starts in our hearts, it gets ordered in our minds, but it must find expression in our hands. Please do something in response to what you have learned in this book! Ultimately God is honoured and the world is changed when truth becomes transformation.

Together with you in Christ,

Dion Forster
Cape Town